Andy Costello has been a Catholic priest for over 50 years. He became a priest to become a missionary in Brazil – but his religious community, the Redemptorists, started him off in the East Village of Manhattan New York City. It was right at the time of the hippie revolution. He has since served in New Jersey, Pennsylvania, Wisconsin, Ohio, Washington D.C., Maryland and a lot of other places.

To the many folks in many churches who stretched me
with their insights and their questions.

Andy Costello

I Am a Catholic in Case of an Accident

AUSTIN MACAULEY PUBLISHERS®

LONDON ∗ CAMBRIDGE ∗ NEW YORK ∗ SHARJAH

Ordering Information
Quantity sales: Special discounts are available on quantity purchases by corporations, associations, and others. For details, contact the publisher at the address below.

Publisher's Cataloging-in-Publication data
Costello, Andy
I Am a Catholic in Case of an Accident

ISBN 9798891551794 (Paperback)
ISBN 9798891551817 (ePub e-book)
ISBN 9798891551800 (Audiobook)

Library of Congress Control Number: 2024912034

www.austinmacauley.com/us

First Published 2024
Austin Macauley Publishers LLC
40 Wall Street, 33rd Floor, Suite 3302
New York, NY 10005
USA

mail-usa@austinmacauley.com
+1 (646) 5125767

Table of Contents

I Am a Catholic
In Case of an Accident

"I am a Catholic."

"If you're a Catholic, would you hesitate to admit it?"

If someone asked, "Do you have a religion?" I would simply answer, "Yes."

Some people might reply, "Right now, I don't – but I did once."

I'm 84. When we were kids, I noticed small cards in prayer books and desk drawers that had on them the words "*I am a Catholic. In case of an accident, please call a priest.*" I don't remember if there was a period or a comma after the word 'Catholic'.

My mother was hit by a car in a hit-and-run accident on April 7, 1987. She was 82 years old. She was walking to church on a Tuesday morning when a car came rushing down 6th Avenue in Brooklyn, New York. The car was heading into the morning sun. The driver didn't see my mother crossing the avenue. She was hit by the car and it kept going. Someone ran toward my mother, looked at her, called 911, and then called the church. A priest came running up the street, said some prayers over her bloody body, and anointed her with sacred oil.

An ambulance arrived in 10 minutes. She had been thrown into the air and landed on her head. They took her to Lutheran Hospital. They worked on her, especially her brain, but she was pronounced dead at 12 noon. I received the call in upstate New York and arrived in Brooklyn by 11:30 AM. I waited outside the operating room, only to be told around noon that she didn't survive. Because of all this, at that time, I found myself in what I would call a 'faith time'. I was in a time of finding out. I was in a time with family. I was in a time of 'Oh no'! I was in a time of learning.

On Being a Catholic

At that time, I was a Catholic. I still am.

Being Catholic is a way of seeing. It's a way of being. It's a way of doing life.

I don't have to explain why I am Catholic. I was born into this way of life, and I continue to choose it now. Over time, questions have arisen within me. Don't we all have questions? Don't we? Once, I was with a group of priests from Richmond, Virginia. They discovered that I was a member of a group of men called the 'Redemptorists'. Several of them informed me that they knew a priest in my congregation from a long time ago, whom everyone went to for confession. They then added, "No matter what sin you confessed, he would simply say, 'Don't we all, don't we all.'"

I'm a member of it all. I've always liked to say, "I'm also a member of the human race." In fact, that's a fundamental truth. Accepting and understanding that can bring about immense happiness and valuable insights, provoking questions and providing some answers.

I like wearing T-shirts with messages on them. It's often the key that opens doors and starts conversations. Like today I'm wearing a red T-shirt with the words 'Bay of Fundy' on it. Two people asked, "Where's that?"

Who, what, when, where, why, and how are great human questions that everybody asks.

If you're reading this book, I hope the word 'Catholic' grabbed your attention. I hope you're aware that you ask basic questions like "Who am I?" and "Why am I the way I am?" and "How did I get to my wheres and whens?"

Being Catholic…how did that come about? If Catholic, why do I remain Catholic? Or why am I on hold? Or why have I dropped out? Who? What? When? Where? Why? How?

Hearing One or Two
of the Following

When I hear any of the following comments, do I hear a lot of different things?

- I used to go to Church.
- I think our family used to go to church.
- I am a Catholic.
- We still go to Church – not every Sunday – but maybe half of the time.
- We're Protestant.
- I'm a Buddhist
- I'm spiritual.
- I believe in God.
- I think about these things – some of the time.
- I have values.
- Sorry, I'm somewhere else right now.

My ears perk up – when religion or religious comments are mentioned in restaurants or at the dining room table.

I especially hear people when they say on TV Talk Shows – "I'm Catholic." Or "I used to be Catholic, but…"

I want to know the rest of the story. I want to hear the other side of the but. It's probably because I'm a priest and because I'm from a Catholic family – and lately because the next generation of our family – seem to have dropped out of the church – and moved away from Church stuff.

Wondering about them – and having heard so many old people like me – bringing up the 'religion' and 'faith' questions – I began writing this book.

I'm interested in where it will take me.

Maybe you are too. Hope this book triggers good stuff for you.

People

People have questions, forget answers, wonder about sport scores, love Oreos, like to visit state parks, like the sound of trains, haven't ridden a bike in 35 years, constantly talk about the weather, simply love raspberry jam, like to knit, do jigsaw puzzles, sculpt, give away old hard bread turning green to the birds, get angry, get lost, play cards, like peanut butter, eat apples, mandarins, bananas, donuts, tacos, do crossword puzzles, know the value of WD-40 and duct tape, have band-aids handy, keep the glove compartment of their car neat – as well as the trunk, go to church at times, also visit art museums, still use $20 bills, cash, stop at night before going into the house to see the moon when it's full, laugh, say "Thank you," visit the elderly, begin over and over again, some use handkerchiefs, some use paper tissues, some never walk by a piano without playing a note, like to have a good pair of scissors at hand, say to themselves, "Someday I'll be using a cane," bite their nails, always listen to music on their car radio, tap their fingers on church benches, love cold water with ice cubes in the glass, check the color of other people's eyes, wonder what day or days of the week they pick up the garbage on this street, always read what's written on street metal sewer covers, also always read what's written on coffee cups, love chocolate chip cookies, know where there is a strong hammer in their house, can change a car tire, get nervous when they spot a snake or a tiger, did well in math and geography in grade school, would still try to jump rope if given the chance, pick up paper clips, you never know, wash out soda cans before tossing them, prefer wooden floors, consider themselves liberal, would kill a mosquito if they saw one, like the sound of a bouncing basketball on a macadam outside court, enjoy house painting, like a quiet snowfall, think there is no age limit for flying a kite, pray, love to ride on a ferry boat, sing when everyone is singing "Happy birthday," go to funerals, and know you don't have to say anything, just be there, like to walk in summer rain without an umbrella or a raincoat, are not hesitant to try a yo-yo, love ice cream (most flavors), remember their first bicycle, like to dance, would take gum when offered, never smoked a cigarette in their life, got drunk once, never read obituaries, could find a pencil with a pink top eraser in their house in less than a minute, are usually early for movies, church, and restaurants, never burp, in fact think that is a bad habit, save photographs, like celebrating others' birthdays but not their own, etc., etc., etc.

Blue Wrist Band

"PROUD TO BE CATHOLIC."

Cost: $1.99.

It's like a rubber band – certainly not worth $2.

I bought it because I could use it for a chapter in this book.

I've been wearing it, wondering if anyone will notice it and ask about it.

I've been thinking about the word 'proud'. I'll explore that theme as well as the meaning of 'Catholic' throughout this book.

'Proud' is an interesting word with both positive and negative connotations.

In the positive sense, proud can mean feelings of joy, being blessed, or being lucky.

In the negative sense, proud can mean feeling superior or thinking that I'm better than you.

A proud person can be described as having their nose in the air, being arrogant, and feeling superior.

I'll continue wearing this wristband to see if I receive any interesting comments or questions.

I don't think I'd put this message on my car as a bumper sticker.

I wouldn't wear it printed on the front of a T-shirt, facing you.

But I'll continue to wear it on my wrist, waiting to see what kind of reactions and questions it might elicit.

So right now, I'm proud to be wearing a blue wristband that says "PROUD TO BE CATHOLIC." Let's see what happens next.

Catholic Last Names

I tend to think that some last names indicate a person is Catholic more than others with different last names.

That's silly – because I've been wrong so many times when I assumed someone is Catholic based on their last name, and they weren't.

Like Italians, Irish, and Polish people…

I do the same with Muslim names, assuming the person is Muslim.

I assume that Norwegian and Swedish last names are Lutheran.

As time goes on, I believe that this assumption on my part will become less true.

Marriage certainly changes many stories. People convert or change their religion because of their spouse. Religion can be a tricky situation, or it can become one. Who influences the other more: the wife or the husband?

Where this becomes relevant to me is when someone commits a crime or does something terrible that makes the news. If the person's name sounds Catholic to me, I feel disappointed because I always hope that religion – especially Catholicism – influences people's moral lives.

The same feeling arises when a relative with the same last name as me gets arrested. If their name appears in the news, I want to hide.

If someone is Catholic in name only, 'bah humbug'.

I expect Catholics to be Catholic for more meaningful reasons than mere chance.

But as I contemplate all of this, I realize that I need to do my research and read about all the issues involved. I need to ask myself, "Why Catholic?"

Is Religion Worth Fighting About?

When I hear people criticizing Catholicism I get ticked off at times.

How about you?

I want to say out loud, "There are plenty of things you can criticize in Catholicism; there are plenty of things you can praise."

If the heavy duty critic is an ex-Catholic, what's the story?

Maybe they haven't thought it over. Maybe they have no desire to vent their complaints. Maybe they haven't figured it out how to deal with unmet expectations. Have they ever heard the line in one of Hafiz's poems, "Get the blame straight."

Do they have ideas, opinions, or comments about rituals, religions, going to church, mosque, or synagogue?

Do they discuss religion with others?

Have they met holy people?

Do they pray?

Have they had any God experiences in their life?

Do they believe in life after death?

Have they ever had in hand writings or books that are considered sacred?

If they were in a car on a Sunday morning – they are stopped at a red light – and 500 people are coming out of church – what would be their thoughts?

It's Thanksgiving week and they read in a local paper that a Catholic high school raised enough money for 500 Thanksgiving dinners for the poor and the hungry in the area. What would be their thoughts after hearing that?

On Being a Priest

What's it like to be a Catholic priest?

Robert Fulghum – author of *Everything I Learned, I Learned in Kindergarten*, says, "If asked while seated on a plane what I do for a living?"

I say, "Oh I'm a neurosurgeon" – this is, if I want to stay quiet.

What would it be like to say, "Oh I am a priest."

That's an interesting answer.

Ask and you'll get interesting answers – and some answers will surprise you. They will tell you – as you listen – various things about the explainer.

Right here…right now – let me go this way: Being a priest for almost 60 years now, I have been called many times to pray with and for someone who was dying – sometimes surrounded by their family – a few times in serious accidents like my mom's.

It can be quite a moment.

I don't know if I'd mention what happened to my mom.

It's an energy filled moment when receiving the Sacrament of the Sick. Back when I was a kid, that ceremony or sacrament was called 'Extreme Unction' – because it was mainly for the dying – at the extreme end of their life. For some, that's still their main idea about this sacrament.

Around the time of the Second Vatican Council – which went from 1962 till 1965 – this sacrament – this sacred ceremony – was changed to a new title *Sacrament of the Sick*.

Moreover, one could receive the sacred oil – the sacred anointing – for various other reasons and times – than the time of death.

Some understood the change in the title. Some didn't. Today there are still folks around who only see it as the sacrament one receives when one is about to die. As a result, they only call for a priest in extreme situations – because they don't want to scare someone who is quite sick.

The title of this book comes from that earlier experience – calling for a priest when one is dying.

It's at that moment some people acknowledge to themselves or for a sick person that they are Catholic – and they want all the help they can get – especially at the time of dying which can be very scary.

The title of this book comes from the experience of an accident or a serious sickness – when a person knows who they are: a Catholic. They also know they want God at the moment – because they are scared to death.

However, in this book I mainly want to get into the meaning of being a Catholic – in this life – before one is dying.

Hopefully, the title of this book is catchy. Hopefully, the title is a fish hook. In fact, I would like to catch you if you are a Catholic – to consider and reconsider the meaning of that title of *I am a Catholic*.

I would like to explore life – all of life – as I said – as well.

Hey, I'm being honest. Hey I'm being transparent. Okay, I'm also being cute with my title.

Tragedy – and also comedy can get us to be quite serious.

What's going on – down deep – in our soul right now – today?

I'm saying, "I assume being a Catholic helps."

What are your thoughts about that assumption?

Religion

I like the following definition of religion: "Recognition of God and acting accordingly."

That definition could include Baptists, Methodists, Jehovah's Witnesses, Catholics, Muslims, Sikhs, Hindus, Jews, and various other groups.

Religions have sacred places, sacred books, and religious leaders.

I also like the description of religion as: what we wrap our life around. This comes from seeing or hearing the word 'ligaments' in the word 'religion'.

'Ligamentum' is the Latin word for band or cord – those tough tissues that connect our bones and keep our inner organs in place.

Everyone has ideas and interests – which can keep us connected. When we learn about and from each other, we can discover that our lives are very interesting.

Are there statistics for how often and how many times a person switches religions in their life? If there are, where could you find such statistics?

'Conversion'…'Conversions'…do most people think of 'religion' when they hear the word 'conversion' in any of its forms? Of conversion from sin? Would everyone think some things are sinful – or wrong?

Religious experiences? Who are the people who have had religious experiences?

Would most people get nervous if they sat next to a stranger on a plane and the topic of religion somehow came up?

When I die, what kind of service or remembrance would I want, if any?

Do I have a specific prayer that I look at and pray every once in a while?

I Ams

I read somewhere: *"It's a good idea to take a piece of paper and jot down '10 I ams'."*

For about 30 years, I tried that with individuals and groups. I found out it's a good discussion starter.

Try it on yourself. '10 I ams'.

Then I read someone saying it's a good idea to ask people to come up with '25 I ams'.

Try it. It can even be better than just '10 I ams'.

For the 25 – someone said, "People run out of 'I ams' around 16."

It's then – because of that pause – someone might say something about themselves, they haven't thought of before.

Someone might say, "I am the youngest in a family of six, but also, 'I'm lazy' or 'I am lonely' or 'I am scared of dying'."

I'm asking in this book – whether I would say, "I am a Catholic," when describing myself.

I would also ask, "Looking at your 'I ams', what is the most significant 'I am'?"

Put them in order of significance. Weigh them.

Looking at my 'I ams', in a counseling session, could lead to some very significant revelations.

I am a story.

I am a history.

What's my education history?

What's my work history?

What's my hurt history?

I am a string of relationships.

List them in order of importance.

I am a joiner of groups. I could tell others the groups I have belonged to.

I am a Redemptorist – that's a group of about 5,000 men – around the world – who make vows to each other to work together for a common mission – especially for the poor – people nobody is rushing to serve.

I am a citizen of the United States. I'm now on my third passport – this last one expired in 2023.

I belong to other groups – but not too many with specific indicators like being a Redemptorist.

Take out your wallet! What information can be found in there about the groups you belong to?

I was never a Boy Scout. Do Eagle Scouts have a certificate they could keep in their wallet?

In other words, I am a lot.

Talk to me. Tell me your story.

Edward The Carpenter

Way back when – on the west coast of Ireland – in County Galway – at least that's the way I heard the story – there was a man named Edward the Carpenter.

He was the earliest known family member in our family.

"Edward the Carpenter…"

I like that name.

I assume he was Catholic – because Galway, Ireland was Catholic and I'm Catholic – and my mom and dad were Catholics with roots in Galway, Ireland.

With my imagination, I like to think that there was someone way back when, perhaps Edward the Carpenter, who they started to go to Catholic Mass with seriousness. Those people are my roots.

Maybe it was Edward the Carpenter, or Martin the Farmer, or Mary the Mom, or Barbara the Baker, or Brendan the Thatcher, or Nora the Store Keeper. I would like to know someone with a name who started us on the long line of those going to the local Catholic Church and passed the faith down to us.

Thank you – whoever you were.

I assume it was many, many, many, many generations ago.

Today, when I see people in my family drop out of the Catholic Church, I wonder what they will answer, if asked the Religion Question – when being brought to a hospital – in case of an accident – or sickness.

Would they be interested in hearing that Michael Costello, our dad, and their grandfather was anointed at Moses Maimonides Medical Center – in Brooklyn, New York – a week before he died – on June 26th, 1970? I was the priest who anointed him, with some of our family present.

I remember hearing a priest say in a sermon, "Picture a little kid waking up around 11 at night, having to go to the bathroom. Quietly, she goes by her parents' bedroom. The door is open and a small light is on. She spots her dad, with his back to her, kneeling at his bed saying a night prayer."

Then the preacher said, "I would think that moment has a greater impact on the religious upbringing of that child than all the moments she might have in religion classes or church services for the rest of her life."

When I heard that, I thought to myself, *Exaggeration.*

However…

My mom and dad used to go to our parish church, Our Lady of Perpetual Help, a Catholic Church in Brooklyn, New York, when we were growing up. I assume their parents went to the local Catholic Church in Ballynahown, County Galway, Ireland, when they were growing up.

And back and back and back and back till Edward the Carpenter.

I don't know the facts or the stories, but here I am, still a Catholic, whose roots may trace back to someone named 'Edward the Carpenter' or perhaps someone named 'Mary the Baker' or 'Evelyn the Knitter'.

So I wonder if those who have stopped going to church think about these things and what is to come.

When I was a kid, I was an altar boy. One weekday, while serving the 6 A.M. Mass, I looked out at the people in the church pews attending Mass, and I spotted my dad kneeling there in church.

It was a surprise because I knew he usually went to work at 5 AM. Well, for some reason, that day, he would be getting into work at Nabisco, over on the West Side of Manhattan, later that morning.

Seeing my dad in church by accident that weekday morning, along with so many other people, must have had some impact on me.

Life. How do we become who we become? Ah, the sweet mystery of life – how do or did we become who we have become so far…

Stan Musial
The Baseball Player

About ten years ago I received in the mail a major league baseball with one autographed name on it: 'Stan Musial'.

I had mentioned in a Sunday sermon for some reason that Stan Musial – a left-handed hitter – was a great hitter to left field. It should have been right field.

One of the persons at Mass that morning knew a few things about Stan Musial that I didn't know. He's the guy who sent me the autographed baseball.

I had heard in a documentary TV program that Stan Musial was from Donora, Pennsylvania. The baseball field they played at basically had no right field. A steep hill went down right behind 2nd base to 1st base.

So you better hit to left field – otherwise there would be a big delay in the game – to recover any baseball that went down that hill in right field.

I don't know what the point was in my sermon. Maybe I was saying that we do lots of things we don't know why we are doing them. It might be interesting to discover the reasons for the twists and turns of our life.

I probably mentioned in my sermon that Ken Griffey Jr. – another great Hall of Fame lefty hitter was also from Donora, Pennsylvania like Stan Musial.

I don't know how skilled Ken Griffey was as an opposite field hitter – or where he played baseball as a kid.

Whatever…

So by saying what I said in my sermon, I received a baseball in the mail – signed by Stan the Man Musial.

The person who sent it to me also informed me that an autographed baseball with Stan Musial's name on it, is the most popular autographed baseball there is.

And the reason for that is this: a group of Catholic men in St. Louis, Missouri came up with the idea of giving a baseball with Stan Musial's autograph – to any boy who attended Sunday Mass.

That meant they had to approach Stan the Man Musial to go along with this. He did.

I added that part of the story to my Stan Musial narrative.

I'd like to add, "I wonder if there is any Catholic man in the United States who has attended church for the rest of his life simply because he received a Stan Musial baseball."

I also added: "Does anyone really know why they do what they do and why?"

Wait a minute! I need to think about that.

Why did I put this piece of information in this book?

Why People Stop Going to Mass?

I would think people know why they stopped going to Mass more than why they continued going to Mass.

I was visiting some people one Christmas and being a priest I asked how the Christmas sermon was. I knew they were Catholic.

I didn't expect their answer: "Oh, we stopped going to Mass."

Silence…

Not expecting that comment, I said sort of nervously, "What happened?"

"We were sick and tired of hearing sermon after sermon from our priest attacking gays."

He continued, "He's repeating himself more and more and more."

I said, "There are other churches."

Silence.

Maybe it became too much of the same old same old for them.

How many people have stopped going to Mass for reasons like that?

What are the numbers like after the child abuse crisis in the Catholic Church?

What are the numbers like after the Corona virus?

What was it like in the Catholic Church after the Protestant Reformation?

I've had one-on-one calls and meetings with some people who dropped out of going to church.

Sometimes some people come back; sometimes nope they don't.

At weddings, baptisms and funerals, I look around and wonder about people sitting off to the side. I don't know their story. I don't know their background. If they are Catholic, are they still church goers?

I don't know.

But as a priest – I wonder how many people have stopped going to Mass because of me.

I wonder and worry about that.

I hope and hope and hope!

At the last supper question, Jesus said, "One of you will betray me!"

The disciples looked at each other thinking and wondering – "Who is he talking about?"

Judas asked, "Is it I Lord?"

"It is at times."

"That's an 'Uh oh'!"

When giving week end retreats, I've heard people say, "I can tell when my priest has gone on a priest's retreat. His sermons are better for at least three weeks in a row."

I've told priests that during priest's retreats – and I can hear their silent reaction to that comment.

It's often a semi-Uh oh!

Maureen

My brother, Billy, once told me that he went to a church on the other side of town one Sunday morning. It wasn't the usual Catholic Church he attended.

During the sermon, he found himself looking around the church and spotted his daughter 15 rows ahead of him, off to the left.

Surprising.

At that time, she was about 17 years old and still living at home.

What is it like to see your daughter at Sunday Mass in a church other than the one the family goes to?

Interesting.

It reminded me of a story a man once told me. His daughter came to the church where I was stationed to get married. I met with her and her fiancé, and their names and wedding date were recorded in the book.

However, they ended up breaking up before the wedding.

A few years later, she called again and came in with her new fiancé. They chose a date and proceeded with the steps toward their marriage.

During the wedding reception, I happened to strike up a conversation with her dad on the side. He told me something I didn't know before. He said, "Every father who has a daughter looks forward to the moment he walks her down the aisle at her wedding, always."

Then he added, "I almost didn't make it to this one today. When she was 15, I was diagnosed with cancer, and it was terminal. Well, I told God, "No! It doesn't work that way." And sure enough, the treatments worked, and here I am today."

Surprising. Not only did he get to walk his daughter down the aisle on that day, but two years later, he walked down the aisle again with his wife, daughter, son-in-law, and their first-born baby for her baptism into the Christian faith.

Just like my brother seeing his daughter, Maureen, in church, I, as a priest, am also blessed with wonderful moments.

My brother has seven daughters, and as a priest, I have officiated four of their weddings.

As a human being, I love observing people's faces at weddings, baptisms, graduations, birthdays, and Friday night high school football games – all of life's gatherings.

Life is about coming together with others and discovering their hopes and surprises.

We need connection, community, celebration, and, as a priest, I would add, church.

As a priest, I have also heard many fathers, mothers, and others express sadness about their children and grandchildren not attending church or getting married in a church. They often ask, "What will they do? Who will they turn to when they need God in their lives?"

For example, in times of accidents…

You Still Believe in That Stuff?

From time to time I've met people who said to me, "You mean to say, you still believe in that religion stuff?"

I consider that comment to be an insult – but being a priest – I pause and hold back comments – yet comments often echo in my inner room.

I call these echoes 'Thinkings'.

I wonder which is the better move: to challenge the other or to remain quiet.

The other sometimes seems to be saying: "I would think you're a thinking person, therefore I think you're not thinking here…"

I would love to ask them if they have ever heard of Bernard Lonergan.

I once got a call as priest to come and pray with and anoint a woman named Roberta Hart – who was on her death bed. It was a rich and wonderful moment.

This time I got a book and not a baseball.

Just before I left her house after anointing her, she asked her son to go to a closet in her bedroom. It was filled with books. She directed him to get a big fat book entitled, *Insight*. Its subtitle was *A Study of Understanding*. It was a 875-page paperback – Volume 3 of the Collected Works of Bernard Lonergan.

We were introduced to the thoughts of this Canadian Jesuit priest way back in the 1960s when we were studying theology. I must admit that he is a tough read.

Roberta took the book from her son and handed it to me. She said, "I took a workshop by Lonergan years ago. Great stuff. I guess I'm not going to finish this book – but I hope you will."

She handed it to me. I'm still working on it.

Why am I telling you this story – and mentioning this man Bernard Lonergan?

Well, I love books and I know some books. I want to ask people who don't think theology is thought provoking, if they have done any thinking in the world of theology.

I would like to know where they got their thinking from – where they got their beliefs from – where and what their assumptions are.

Do they ever stop to think that others think differently?

I once got a life lesson that I spotted in a Charlie Brown Peanuts' cartoon. I just looked it up on Goggle and there it was after all these years. It must have hit other people as well.

Lucy, Linus and Charlie are standing there on a green grass hill. They are looking up at the clouds.

Lucy begins by asking, "Aren't the clouds beautiful? They look like big balls of cotton..."

The three of them lay down on the grass – looking up into the sky at the clouds.

Lucy says, "If you use your imagination, you can see lots of things in the cloud formations..."

Then she asks, "What do you see, Linus?"

Linus responds, "Well, those clouds up there look like the map of British Honduras on the Caribbean…that cloud up there looks a little like the profile of Thomas Eakins, the famous painter and sculptor…and that group of clouds over there gives me the impression of the stoning of Stephen…I can see the apostle Paul stand there to one side…"

Lucy says, "Uh huh…that's very good. What do you see in the clouds, Charlie Brown?"

Charlie says, "Well, I was going to say I saw a ducky and a horsie, but I changed my mind!"

That story can be found in *The Complete Peanuts* 1959 –1960.

I would like to tell those people who think I'm an intellectual loser to read Charles Schulz – his books – his cartoons – and his theology.

If they are not Catholic, I might ask if they grew up in a specific religion and if they ever did their homework on and about that faith vision.

I also want to tell them to read Thomas Berry and James Martin and Richard Rohr and Elizabeth Johnson and Krista Tippett and 100 others.

I want them to read the poems of Mary Oliver and Seamus Heaney.

I wish they would keep their eyes open for a lecture on God or religion or humanism at a local church or college.

I would then suggest they subscribe to a Catholic magazine like *America* or *Commonweal* or *U.S. Catholic* or *Liguorian*,

I guess what I really want to do is shut them up and get them to say what I once read in the Talmud: "Teach thy tongue to say, 'I do not know.'"

Some folks really don't know anything about religions – but they make comments about religion.

Why do people do that?

More intriguing: do they know that about themselves – that they do that?

Jesus The Carpenter

When it comes to religion, I'm proud to say that I am a follower of Jesus Christ.

I am a follower of Jesus the Carpenter – as well as Edward the Carpenter.

Jesus liked to walk.

He liked to talk with people.

He carved out some great sentences – said some memorable words. He gave folks some profound ways to figure out how to deal with life.

Jesus gave life meaning.

Jesus was a wise figure.

I also believe that he is God.

Now that's a significant leap of faith.

Catholics and Christians in general take great leaps of faith.

I make incredible leaps: seeing Jesus as both human and divine.

I have heard people passing judgments on others based on how they live their lives, including the number of children they have or where they reside. They label these individuals as stupid, wrong, or foolish.

Two generations ago, people used to say, "Catholics have too many kids."

My brother and his wife have seven daughters, and I am happy that they have all seven. I believe they share the same belief.

Some people do not inquire about others' beliefs or how they arrived at them. Instead, they jump in with their prejudices and beliefs. They do not examine their own hearts, minds, or thoughts.

They do not know the origins of the ingredients in their own soup.

I have read the four primary accounts of the life of Jesus Christ, known as the 4 Gospels – Matthew, Mark, Luke, and John – many times.

The Gospels and others gave me my thoughts about Jesus.

I went to Catholic School.

I obtained three Master's Degrees in religious fields, which taught me about various religious teachings.

Becoming a Christian or a Catholic begins with receiving a 'Credo–A creed'. It is a list of fundamental beliefs.

A Credo is a list of essential teachings of a specific religious faith.

If you continue reading this book, you will come across mentions of these basic creeds.

Three early Christian creeds are the Apostles' Creed, the Nicene Creed, and the Chalcedonian Creed.

I also believe that people have personal creeds, which consist of beliefs, opinions, and ideas about life that they have acquired throughout their lives.

I believe it would be beneficial to write down one's beliefs.

I think it would be good to sit with another person or others and clarify one's basic beliefs.

It would also be a good idea to make a list of questions.

In fact, if you find yourself not changing many periods at the end of your sentences into question marks, maybe you have a cluttered mind.

Quotes About Being
a Catholic

"If you're going to do a thing, you should do it thoroughly. If you're going to be a Christian, you may as well be a Catholic." Muriel Spark (1918–2006) in *Independent,* August 2, 1989

"Gentlemen, I am a Catholic. As far as possible, I go to Mass every day. This [taking a rosary out of his pocket] is a rosary. As far as possible, I kneel down and tell these beads every day. If you reject me on account of my religion, I shall thank God that He has spared me the indignity of being your representative." (Someone in some book I read).

"He was of the faith chiefly in the sense that the church he currently did not attend was Catholic." Kingsley Amis (1922–1995) in *One Fat Englishman* (1963), Chapter 8.

"You have no idea how much nastier I would be if I was not a Catholic. Without supernatural aid I would hardly be a human being." Evelyn Waugh (1903–1966) in Noel Annan *Our Age* (1990)

"Once a Catholic always a Catholic." Angus Wilson (1914–1991) in *The Wrong Set* (1949) p. 168

"There are not one hundred people in the United States who hate The Catholic Church, but there are millions who hate what they wrongly perceive the Catholic Church to be." Fulton J. Sheen

"I was brought up as a Catholic and went to church every week and took the sacraments. It never really touched the core of my being." Sting

"Sometimes I regret not being Catholic. I think I'd make a pretty good saint." Zach Braff

"Try imagining James Joyce not writing about being a Catholic." Victor LaValle

"I just try to be the best Catholic." Stephen Colbert

"For me, being Catholic was who I was and who I am, just like I'm Irish and Slovak. It's just so ingrained in us." Regina Brett

"I think being a Catholic made me a better person. It taught me how to choose good over evil, and how to be a more caring human being." Sonia Sotomayor

"The beauty of Catholicism is every human being's right." Matthew Kelly

"The Catholic men are more upset about women not being able to be priests than are Catholic women." Andrew Greeley

"You never stop being Catholic. It's like the Mafia or Amway." Tim Dorsey

"I have a lot of mental scars from being brought up Catholic and being sent to Catholic school for 13 years!" Mat McNerney

"Being a Catholic is the most important aspect of my life." Mark Wahlberg

"To be Catholic is the only way of being fully and utterly Christian." Pierre Teilhard De Chardin

"The Catholic Church is the only thing which saves a man from the degrading slavery of being a child of his age." G.K. Chesterton

"You know you are Catholic when someone asks you your favorite Madonna song and you say 'Hail Holy Queen'."

"It is the test of a good religion whether you can joke about it." G, K. Chesterton

"Each generation is converted by the saint who contradicts it the most." G. K. Chesterton

"Just going to church doesn't make you a Christian any more than standing in your garage makes you a car." G. K. Chesterton

On Going to Mass

It was midsummer – August something.

It was a Saturday afternoon and a mom and dad were planning to go to Mass the next morning, but where?

They were on vacation with their 5 kids and the kids didn't have a say or a vote. They were too young for that. Besides, this was the early 1960s.

They were somewhere in Lower Virginia, headed for a state park with a lake. It was the good old days – way back when.

They asked around if anyone knew where a Catholic Church was. Nobody knew. Nobody was Catholic.

They found a phone book with the name of a Catholic Church. They called and got a voice. It was Father Mike.

"We'd love to have you…tomorrow morning at 10:30. We're not too crowded. Do you know where we are and how to get here?"

Dad said, "We'll be there. We have maps. You'll see all 7 of us at 10:30. We're a Catholic family on vacation from the Wyoming Valley in Pennsylvania."

"Great…looking forward to meeting you – and to celebrating Mass with you on a Sunday morning. It's supposed to be a nice day."

Twenty-five years later, the whole family decided to take that same vacation again. All 7 – but now they were 12, with two marriages and mom and dad with 5 grandkids.

Throughout the years, they would tell the story of going to a wonderful Mass on a Sunday morning way down in southern Virginia.

They found the place. It was quite easy, just off the main highway.

They would say, "There were only 15 people there. Our 7 made it 22."

We were introduced. Everyone said, "Hello!" to everyone else.

We were invited to lunch afterwards. "Everyone went. Everyone wanted to know who everyone was. Great potato salad."

"That's all – but we considered it the best Mass we had ever attended."

Then the mom said, "We think – you're not going to believe this – this is why our kids and now their families have gone to Mass all these years."

"Just one Mass. Wow, we were appreciated as Catholics – and vice versa."

"And surprise – now, 25 years later – Father Mike is still alive, but in a nursing home. It's close by and we went to see him – and thank him for that Mass – way back when."

Other than that, they couldn't explain why this happened.

They knew neighbors and friends – who had stopped going to church – for various reasons, known and unknown.

They knew going to Sunday Mass was their identity. It was as simple as that.

It was as simple as that.

Glass Library Door

In late August of 1960 I arrived at a major seminary in Esopus, New York. It was to further my education in becoming a priest.

On the first day there – I walked down to the library – stood at the entrance – and before entering I looked through two glass doors.

I could see a big enormous room – open in the center – with a high, high ceiling. Along the sides it had 4 floors of books.

I had 6 years to check out the books in that room.

The first floor – ground zero – had Catholic Magazines – bound.

The second floor had Patrology and Scripture books – as well as psychology and philosophy.

The third floor had theology.

The fourth floor had literature and a section called 'Hell'.

Hell was condemned books – and it was locked.

The 4 floors – like balconies – had stairs – leading up and up to the 4th floor.

By 1967 – after I graduated – after I was ordained a priest – I can say I knew that library. I did sneak into "Hell" a few times. No big deal.

A significant change took place in the mid-1960 – when Catholic and Protestant books were placed side by side on the shelves – mainly Catholic.

If one of us was doing a term paper on Baptism – we would be reading what different scholars of different denominations – would have written on that topic or theme.

In time I also got to dabble more and more in the bound magazine section of the library on the first floor.

In our classrooms we began in 1960 with 3 sets of key textbooks: *Barbadette* for philosophy; *Herve* for dogmatic theology; and *Aertnes/Damen* for moral theology. These 3 sets of text books were in Latin and we were there to master the material.

The first two years in the major seminary was our last two years of college and we had 2 volumes of *Barbadette* for philosophy. To know Philosophy with its different branches was the goal. We also had courses in sociology and history, some Greek and Spanish.

The first two years after college we had dogmatic theology with all its branches. Add catechetic and Old Testament and various other courses.

And the last two of those 4 years of post-college education we had moral theology and New Testament and various other courses.

The library supplemented those 6 years – the last 2 years of college and then the 4 years of post-college classes and courses.

Half way through those 6 years in this major seminary the most significant moment was the Second Vatican Council that took place in Rome.

A closed Catholicism and seminary education – changed.

I remember one teacher saying, "Here is a list of 10 magazine articles to read on this particular topic. There will be thousands more before you die."

Read. Read. Read. Think. Think. Think. Wonder. Wonder. Wonder.

You have a life time of study before you.

We moved from a closed education system to an open ended system – and my mind was ready for the future.

One just had to go down to the library – open up those see through glass doors – walk in and watch how the Catholic Church changed in the 1960s.

Philosophy

When studying to become a Catholic priest, we had 2 years of philosophy as the last 2 years of our 4 years of college.

It was around 1960. I was a B student. I was so-so – when it comes to thinking. Complicating our philosophy courses for me was that our major textbooks were in Latin.

We were taught Scholastic Philosophy – which had evolved since medieval times. The branches were Logic, Metaphysics, Ethics, Theosophy and the History of Philosophy.

Besides taking the courses in Latin, looking back a big weakness was that we didn't take courses in Existentialism and other branches and forms of modern philosophy.

One of the goals of the philosophy courses was to introduce us to scholastic theology and how to study in Latin.

Looking back I slowly realized that I lacked philosophy skills. I also lacked courses in psychology – and anthropology – as well as science.

Living with and listening to other priests I slowly learned that there are two kinds of people: the open-minded and the closed-minded. I also found out that the world is a classroom and the teachers are the people who walk the planet.

Somewhere along the line I read Eartha Kitt's comment, "I am learning all the time, the tombstone will be my diploma."

I learned the importance of attending lectures and talks – reading and hearing life's questions.

Writing is something I also figured out. It was something I wanted to do – and I only have so much time.

Hence this book – and a few others I've written – plus articles – plus the other books I need to finish. There will be more to come. I hope…

Cries But Silent...

I once got a phone call from a guy I know…

He said he was in Chicago and that morning had walked into a used book store. He spotted a book I had written years earlier. It was for 25 cents.

I asked him if he bought it. He said, "No."

About a week later, I got a call from a stranger – who was looking for a book I had written years earlier. I didn't have any copies, so I suggested he check used book stores or eBay.

I rarely get these calls, but I got another one the following week. I gave the same advice.

Then it hit me, "Hey stupid…check out eBay and see if that's a good way to get a book that you've written and it's out of print."

I did. I found one of my books on eBay for about $4.95. Then, to my surprise, I also found a copy of one of my old books online for $228.00. It was the same book that the guy saw in Chicago for 25 cents. I called the guy and told him he should have bought it for 25 cents because it is now selling for $228.00.

I also said to myself, "If I knew that, I would have bought and saved a whole box of them."

I think the book was *Cries But Silent*…I have 5 books published, and this was my favorite.

One book sold about 60,000 copies – a paperback entitled *How To Deal With Difficult People*.

After writing it, I often liked to say, "It doesn't work. It's quite difficult to deal with difficult people." I like to add, "But it was translated into Korean. How's that for bragging rights?"

But it had a good title. Everybody wants to know how to deal with difficult people. How-to books are a great way to go.

So let me try to explain the how of things – how I got to write a few things.

I was at San Alfonso Retreat House in West End, Long Branch, New Jersey. During Holy Week – in Lent – we came up with the idea of speaking on the 7 Last Words of Jesus. We did it again the following three years.

I now had 4 talks – and they were poetic – in verse form. I decided to write 3 more. I now had a manuscript – a small, possible paperback book – which I sent to our Redemptorist publishing house in Liguori, Missouri.

Title? I gave it the title *World's Greatest Crossword Puzzle.*

I thought that was a good title – but the publishers changed the title to *How to Pray When Troubled.*

I thought my title was better – and clever as well. But I was being published. So I was on my way as a writer in 1977 – at the age of 37.

I said to myself, "I guess *How-To* books are the way to go."

So book #2 was *How to Deal With Difficult People.*

My next book, *Listenings*, was rejected by Liguorian – as well as 5 or 6 other publishers.

Good luck…a guy who read my first two books came on retreat to St. Alphonsus Retreat House in Tobyhanna, Pennsylvania. He asked if I had anything else published.
I said, "Rejects."

He then said, "Try Thomas More publishers in Chicago."

So I sent Listenings in on that Monday morning, and I got a call that Wednesday from a guy named Joel Wells. He simply said, "Like it – but could you make it a bit longer?"

I was off and running as a writer again, and they published 4 books. Then they sold the company, and I was on the street again. Life…

'The' and 'A'

Somewhere along the line I learned the difference between 'a' and 'the'.

It's a rather simple and basic distinction.

I was stationed with a priest who tended to make lots of definitive statements.

I slowly started to say to myself about him, "Wait a minute! I wouldn't be that sure about this or that."

He would state the reason why so and so said or did something. "The reason was…"

I'd inwardly think there could be 100 other motives or reasons.

So the one thing I learned from this guy was the difference between 'a' and 'the'.

Then I began wondering if I could formulate a wisdom saying, "There are two kinds of people: a people and the people."

Translation: some people see single solutions – or single answers – to problems and issues; some people see multiple possible solutions to problems and issues.

If you read this book, my hope will be that you'll look at and think about a lot of issues and questions when it comes to religion and being a Catholic. I just want to open up doors – or windows.

At baptisms and weddings and funerals – I find myself looking around at the faces of people – sitting off to the side – or a bit behind the participants – and sometimes I see questions sculpted into their faces.

Sometimes – someone gives me a call – and they ask, "Can we talk?" Sometimes they don't want one answer. Sometimes they know they don't have the answer. Sometimes I simply say, "Do you walk?"

Prudence and The Pill

Years ago my brother Billy said, "If you ever have some girls who would love a summer vacation in Maryland – please let them know – we'd love to have them."

He and his wife had 7 girls.

I was working as a priest in an inner city parish on the Lower East Side of Manhattan at the time.

I asked the mother of two girls and a son from Santo Domingo if the girls would be interested and she said in broken English, "Great – surely – wonderful."

I was able to get the same deal for Willie their brother with a family I knew in Sea Girt, New Jersey.

I brought the two girls – aged 10 and 12 – up to Port Authority Bus Depot – got them tickets – and put them on the bus for Washington D.C.

My brother and two of his girls met them as they got off the bus in D.C.

They had a great 4 weeks with my sister-in-law and their 7 girls – in Laurel, Maryland. They also got to Ocean City, Maryland and experienced some hot, hot summer days in Washington D.C.

One of the funny moments was at a Sunday Mass. My brother and his wife and family were late for Mass – as usual. The parish was just starting – because where they lived was a totally new development. Mass was held in a movie theater – while a church was being built.

That Sunday morning the marquee outside the movie theater had paper covering the name of the movie.

My brother and wife and 9 girls marched down the aisle for the front seats – the only place that had a whole row of almost empty seats. Everyone in the theater watched the 11 heading for the front row.

Of course the guys in the parish couldn't wait until when the Mass was over to bust my brother about the name of the movie *Prudence and the Pill*.

Of course my brother couldn't wait to give me a phone call to tell me the story.

The 4 Gospels in the New Testament are loaded with stories – about things that happened to Jesus and his disciples.

Life is all about story happenings and storytelling.

Willie – the two girls' brother – had a good time in New Jersey – at the ocean – but I'm sure nothing could compare to the adventures his two sisters had with my seven nieces in Maryland.

Thanks to my brother's invitation his daughters saw the value of meeting new people, experiencing hospitality and becoming part of new stories.

I never thought to ask him if anybody else at work tried the same adventure. I'm also sure he couldn't wait to get to work on Monday morning to tell everyone about the movie he didn't see.

Sunday Church Guided Tours

When it comes to church – when it comes to life – when it comes to religion, you never know what's going to grab you.

There was this priest in his mid-fifties – in the mid-west – who came up with a unique way to promote the Catholic religion.

First he did his homework.

He got a 3" X 5" spiral pad and went over to his church on a Wednesday afternoon. He looked around and began jotting down on his pad what he saw in the church.

- altar,
- crucifix
- stations of the cross,
- pulpit,
- stained glass windows,
- statues,
- tabernacle,
- baptismal font,
- lectionary,
- sacramentary,

- Holy Water fonts
- vigil lights – candles
- confession boxes
- sacristy

Small spiral pads are a neat way to keep notes and jot down questions and observations. You can always add more to your notes. You can always get a second and a third pad.

Next, the priest went to his computer and looked up on the Internet search engine everything he could find on different things in the church starting with the altar.

He made each subject a document file and got a loose leaf binder to print out interesting tidbits for each topic.

After he had enough for an hour's presentation, he decided Sunday afternoon at 1 P.M. would be the best time and place for his program.

Next, he told the congregation at all Sunday Masses in February about his plan for Sunday afternoons in March, from 1 PM to 2 PM.

He thought that having 12 people per session would work best. He called the sessions 'Sunday Church Guided Tours'.

In his 2-minute advertisement for Guided Tours after Communion on Sundays, he said, "All questions are allowed. Nothing is off-limits. You should see what's in the sacristy closets and bottom drawers."

"During my sermons, start looking around the church even more – for what you might be interested in."

"There are no stupid questions."

"On the bulletin board in the church vestibule, there are 5 sign-up sheets with 12 available spots."

He concluded his advertisement with the words, "If this works, it works. If it doesn't, we tried."

It worked.

He ended up doing it on Sunday afternoons for 4 months every year.

Other parishes started doing it. Priests talk to each other. People tell each other new and surprising things. People would call up from time to time to ask if they could bring friends to church to give them a guided tour.

They had taken the tour and now they would like to try it.

Some got very good at it – doing their homework – big time.

Some people came back to church as a result.

Some people came into the church as a result.

Some people said, "As a result of this, we always drop into different churches when we are on vacation and check out all the territory."

Some churches have bells up front next to the altar and big bells in the tower if they have one. Little kids on guided tours love to ring them if possible.

Most people, including kids, love to get into the pulpit. If the microphone is turned on at that moment, they love to say something interesting.

Most Catholics don't know about the altar stone underneath the altar cloths and how they have relics embedded in them.

Most priests don't know when church buildings started using altar cloths, where altar rails went after they were removed, and when they started using sanctuary lights in churches.

Priests loved doing this because they got to know their people better and vice versa.

A lady once said she loved coming into an empty church and sitting in the church bench under the 4th station of the cross. She said that her mom loved to do that; it reminded her of her mom. The 4th Station: Jesus meets his Sorrowful Mother. The priest who heard this made it part of his tour – just to mention this – and he often heard people say, "Thank you!" for this suggestion.

A man – a former pro football player – once said, "I love to sit in the back row on the far right whenever I come to church. That's where my mother sat for 23 years – praying for me to come back to church."

Ice cream pops, as a closing treat, in the sacristy refrigerator, was a real winner.

To Be or Not to Become
a Catholic

If someone wants to stop being or becoming a Catholic, there are good reasons to skip out: The abuse scandal doesn't make sense; churchgoers are a bunch of hypocrites.

If someone wants to be or become a Catholic, there are good reasons: I want more of God in my life. I need the Father, Son, and the Holy Spirit in my life. I need a community – a church to belong to – I need a tradition – a meaning system in my life, etc.

Across the street from me right now is a big red Catholic church building: St. Michael's. It has a decent-sized lake next to it. I have been walking around this lake for years now. It's a great walk for health and for thinking.

On Saturday afternoon and on Sunday, I see all the many cars of the people who go to Sunday Mass there. I've wondered what it would be like to survey those folks on why they go to Sunday Mass. It's one of the key ways Catholics announce to themselves and to the world, "I am a Catholic."

I've heard that people like this church because the Mass is relatively short – about 40 to 45 minutes. Going to Mass is a weekly opportunity to say 'Thank You' to God or to ask 'Help' from God. It's an opportunity to hear readings from the Bible and to get a decent 10-minute sermon. If you're a Catholic and you go to Sunday Mass, what are your reasons?

I've heard that some people in Chicago or Philadelphia – when asked where they are from – answer with the name of a parish.

Isn't that interesting? Do they still do that?

I answer, "I'm from Brooklyn." But I'm also proud of coming from Our Lady of Perpetual Help, Brooklyn, New York. Both formed me – getting the most from our church and parish on 5th Avenue between 59th and 60th Street.

I'm still a Catholic, and I'm still a Dodgers fan. I remember Father Rudy Egan, Sister Teresa Carmel 'Tessie', Carl Furillo, and Pee Wee Reese.

Catechisms

When I went to Catholic Grammar School – O.L.P.H. Brooklyn, NY, – for religion classes we used a small paperback book called, *The Baltimore Catechism.*

It had hundreds of questions and answers. It was clear. It was concise. It was made for memorization. It was made for tests.

We were not taught to think. We were taught to know all the answers that were spelled out in black and white. No pictures. Just words.

For me this was 1945–1953.

I have to do my homework on this, but somewhere along the line catechisms changed. Catholic religion courses changed. We humans have an imagination. We love stories. We need illustrations and examples.

So new catechisms arrived in Catholic School classrooms – as well as C.C.D. courses. C.C.D. stands for Confraternity of Christian Doctrine.

The changes had to have happened in Catholic colleges first and teachers started to teach religion differently for Catholic School kids and for religious education classes for Catholic kids in public schools.

Somewhere around 1990 there were complaints about kids not knowing their religion. So in 1992 a new catechism

– The Catechism of the Catholic Church – arrived and it became a cannon ball aimed at our kids and our adults.

It was back to black and white – no pictures – no stories – no examples. As Joe Friday of the TV show, Dragnet, would put it. "Just the facts. Just the facts."

It was big. It was heavy. It did its job of bringing certitude to everyone.

Yet…as an adult, I loved a catechism called 'The Dutch Catechism'. It was like reading a novel at times. It had stories and examples.

Nuns and Sisters

To be Catholic up until the last century, when you heard the word 'nun', you thought of those women who gave their lives for service in the Catholic Church all around the world.

They wore clothing from another time. We saw them in movies like *The Bells of St. Mary's, The Trapp Family Singers*, and *Going My Way*.

We saw them change their clothing after the Second Vatican Council.

They taught us in Catholic schools. They cared for us as nurses in many Catholic hospitals. Some gave their lives in foreign missions for the Church. Some became contemplative sisters behind screens – praying for the world.

We saw them being made fun of in movies. We heard comedy comments like the number of orders of nuns there were is one of the two things God doesn't know. We saw high school and college girls being dressed up as nuns on Halloween. Then there were the strange names of the religious orders of women: Sisters of the Perpetual Adoration of Jesus Christ, etc.

Part of the package of being a Catholic was having nuns or sisters.

I had a sister – my sister Peggy – who was a nun. She joined a group called the Sisters of the Immaculate Heart of Mary. They were founded by a Redemptorist priest: Father Louie Gillet. They divided up into three groups – based on various things like location. My sister's group was in Scranton, Pennsylvania. Another group was in West Chester, Pennsylvania. The third group was in Michigan. They developed their own history and all changed in various ways based on their personalities. Scranton became known as the So So's because they were pictured as the moderates. Detroit was more liberal, so they were called the Go Go's. And the West Chester, PA group were called the No No's.

My dad had 3 sisters who were in the Sisters of Mercy – originally from Ireland. They became nuns as immigrants – after they settled in Portland, Maine. Two died of TB in their 20s and Sister Mary Patrick lived for 50 years – mainly at their motherhouse.

She died on the same day – November 5th – in different years – that my sister Peggy – Sister St. Monica Costello, IHM – died.

I've given many retreats for sisters. Many have colleges and so-called 'Mother Houses' – which serve as office space, training places, headquarters, etc. They all have to have cemeteries. If you ever get a chance to visit a cemetery filled with the graves of sisters, make and take the time to visit them. Stand on the grass. Look at the stones. Read the few words there. Ask, "What was it like?" And listen to autobiography. Amazing.

Priests Say The Darndest Things

A television talk show guy used to say, "Kids say the darndest things." They did and they always will.'

Art Linkletter used to have a TV show that featured funny things kids said.

As a priest, I've heard Catholics tell me things they have heard priests say.

The mentions can be unmentionable. In general, they want me to agree with them – that a certain priest said something pretty stupid.

Jamie told me about a Christmas Mass. At communion time, the priest said right before communion – "If you only come here a few times a year, don't come to communion today."

There was a loud 'GASP' – followed by several 'Oh my God' sounds after that.

After that, people got out of the pews to go to communion and others left the church.

Jamie's son-in-law, who later became a Catholic, said, "Now that wasn't very welcoming, was it?"

Priests get reported from time to time – for things they said or did.

Bishops receive letters and phone calls about their priests.

I don't remember receiving a list of possible infractions or 'No-no's' while going through the seminary – in preparation for becoming a priest. It might not be a bad idea to do just that.

People are either prudent or stupid. Time will tell what kind of person this priest will be.

Time will tell if a priest is willing to learn – to listen – to be for others or for themselves.

I'm now an old man – an old priest – and I'm wondering about the state of the priesthood. Are the clergy of today – modern priests – in this life for the good of others or for their own agenda? I got ordained as a priest in 1965. What were we like compared to the priests of today? I wonder if these recent labels for priests are a new phenomenon: right-wing, left-wing, mechanical, conservative, liberal, normal, rigid, off the wall?

There are boundaries. Priests can't tell if you're going to heaven or to hell. They don't know God's opinion about someone. Who's a saint? Who's a sinner?

Why not capitalize 'sinner' if you capitalize 'saint'?

Priests say the darndest things.

The Inquisition was a dangerous time in the Catholic Church.

Books weren't the only things burned. Sometimes people were.

Names at Baptism

"At baptism, a child had to receive a Catholic saint's first name."

When I hear that, I inwardly ask, "Who made up that rule?"

I also think to myself, "Why on earth would a priest want to engage in that argument?"

I was born on November 10, 1939. November 10 was the feast day of St. Andrew Avellino – so I was given the name Andrew at my baptism. Later on, St. Andrew Avellino was replaced by St. Leo the Great as the feast day on November 10.

I prefer Andrew. I would hate to hear 'The Great'!

But I wonder if the priest who baptized me questioned my dad about the middle name I received at my baptism: Jackson.

I was given the name of the president who is on the twenty-dollar bill. I like that. I have always liked it – and it wasn't because of the twenty-dollar bill.

There's a story behind the name Jackson. Would the priest who baptized me say, "Wow, I like that story – and yes, you can be baptized with the name of a Protestant."

I heard the story when I was in my 30s. Priests in Ireland, in order to encourage vocations to the priesthood in the United States, would mention in Irish pulpits that the 7th president of the United States might have been Catholic if there were more Irish Catholic priests in the United States. So, all you young men out there: think priesthood; think United States.

I like that story.

And I never objected to a name that parents chose for their children.

I'm not crazy.

Telling The Kids

Telling the kids…

Many fathers wonder, "When do I tell my son about the facts of life?"

I'm sure mothers do the same wondering about their daughters.

There are various jokes about that.

The kid already knows. Or, they ask their dad or mom, "What do you want to know?"

Does any parent wonder, "When do I tell my kid about God?"
"When do I tell my kid about religion?"
"When do I tell my kid about church?"

If there is one question parents ask priests, it's the going to church question.

I hear it on every retreat I'm part of. Parents who go to church ask, "What did I do wrong? None of my kids go to church?"

Recently, I noticed a book just sitting there on a table in our retreat house: Tell Me Why. It's by Michael Novak and his daughter Jana Novak. It was the subtitle that got me to pick it up, "A Father Answers His Daughter's Questions About God."

Just reading a book like that for starters – is a good first step.

The work that needs to be done begins with the parents.

We priests have seen thousands of kids brought to church by their parents. Then their kids drop out of church – in their teen years. Dropping out seems to be a 'rite of passage' – like getting one's driver's license – or holding in hand a cold beer – in the bottle or in a can.

We've seen parents bring their kids to church when those kids are making their first confession – but the parents or guardians don't go themselves. Often we say, that's one missed opportunity. Example is a thousand times better than words.

I heard of one Catholic parish that eliminated all their religious education programs for youth – and spent their time, energy, and money on programs to train parents and adults – who would then educate their kids and other young people in our faith – at home.

I heard that – but it was only after mulling that over for months – that I asked, "Did it work?" Too late. I had forgotten where I heard that.

I know the common wisdom saying: "The teacher learns the most."

When I was a parish priest in St. Mary's, Annapolis, Maryland – I went on thirty-plus Kairos retreats with our Catholic high school kids. In that program, the kids themselves give a bunch of the talks. The speaker gets a lot more out of a talk than the listener.

Bottom line: adult education in our faith will take care of a lot of stuff.

Seven Sacraments

If you asked most Catholics how many sacraments there are, I would guess that more than half would say 7.

There are 1 billion, 245 million Catholics in the world. That's 18% of the world's population.

If you asked Catholics to name the 7 sacraments – the number who would know the 7 would be less. One of the purposes of religious education classes would be to get Catholics to know their faith.

Those who want their kids baptized – to receive the sacrament of Baptism – certainly is going down. It's the sacrament that makes a Catholic a Catholic.

If you are a bishop, if you're a pastor of a parish, if you're a parent who goes to Catholic Mass on a regular basis, then you would be concerned about numbers.

As a priest, I hear about this decrease all the time. Lately, more and more parents voice their concerns about their kids not getting married in church.

In case of accidents, sickness, or death arriving at our doorstep, people are not asking for the Sacrament of the Anointing. Add First Communion and Confirmation to that list.

I don't know about the sacrament of confession.

Priests will tell you that the number of single men choosing to become priests is certainly down as well.

We don't know enough about Mass attendance as we still don't know the final report on people attending Mass.

That's the seven sacraments.

I would assume that the bishops of the United States – and then the world – need to do the research on the state of the Faith in our church.

Numbers matter.

Vatican Council III is certainly something that needs to happen – and needs to be called for. Decisions need to be made on a married clergy, women priests – and a lot more major changes all around the world for the Catholic Church.

The Catholic Church has made major changes and shifts in the past. The events and experiences of the past few years certainly scream for major changes as we move into the future.

Come, Holy Spirit.

Rosary Beads

I could see her walking toward me from quite a distance – at least a street and a half away. And the avenue in Manhattan, New York City, where I saw her, was quite crowded.

She was around 45 and well dressed. She had a rosary in hand.

Rosary beads have been a tell for centuries that told us, "Here is a Catholic."

Catholic kids are given a pair of rosary beads when they make their First Communion and at other times in their lives. Kids are taught their Hail Marys early on in life.

At some moment in our childhood, the six of us in our family started saying the Family Rosary together. We would kneel on the wooden floor at our back bedroom bed – Mom, Dad, Billy, Mary, Peggy, and I.

In the 1940s, Father Patrick Peyton began announcing the good news: "The family that prays together stays together." He had another saying that didn't do as well: "A world at prayer is a world at peace."

When I walked into O.L.P.H. church between 59th and 60th street, on 5th Avenue, I would notice people sitting or half-kneeling there, saying the Rosary by themselves in the semi-darkness. Most of the time I'd be heading for the sacristy – up front – near the altars. I was an altar boy.

A rosary had 5 sets of 10 beads. A separate bead separated the 5 mysteries. Hail Marys were said on the 10 beads. An Our Father was said on that single bead before each mystery, and a Glory Be to the Father was said on that same single bead at the end of each of the 5 mysteries.

There were 3 sets of mysteries to pray about and meditate on when I was growing up: The Joyful Mysteries, The Sorrowful Mysteries, and The Glorious Mysteries. Pope John Paul II added another set of mysteries: The Light-Bearing Mysteries in 2002.

You can find these 20 mysteries to reflect on and pray about in many small books of prayers for Catholics.

They are as follows:

The Joyful Mysteries

1. The Annunciation
2. The Visitation
3. The Nativity
4. The Presentation in the Temple

5.   The Finding in the Temple

The Sorrowful Mysteries

1.   The Agony in the Garden
2.   The Scourging at the Pillar
3.   The Crowning with Thorns
4.   The Carrying of the Cross
5.   The Death on the Cross

The Glorious Mysteries

1.   The Resurrection
2.   The Ascension
3.   The Descent of the Holy Spirit
4.   The Assumption of Mary into Heaven
5.   The Crowning of Mary Queen of Heaven

The Luminous or Light Bearing Mysteries

1.   The Baptism of Jesus
2.   The Wedding at Cana
3.   The Proclamation of the Gospel
4.   The Transfiguration
5.   The Eucharist

The idea is to reflect on each of those mysteries while saying the Hail Marys. Catholics who say and pray the Rosary ordinarily say a rosary of 5 decades per day. You can think of Mary or Christ in each decade of the Joyful, the

Sorrowful, the Glorious, or the Luminous mysteries you're praying at the moment.

It's complicated. Over time, the Rosary becomes a part of the person who prays it.

While saying the Rosary, people often have meandering thoughts. Some individuals, when they go to Confession, confess to having distractions while they pray. Priests then tell them that distractions are normal. They might add that you can say the Rosary by yourself or with others – and you can concentrate on the words of the Hail Marys and the Our Father or the Glory Be to the Father. Or you can meditate or space out on the different mysteries and the different sets of five beads in those mysteries.

If you are Catholic, see the Rosary as a gift and give the prayers a try.

About 30 years ago, I started telling people that they can use a pair of Rosary beads for all kinds of prayers. I would say in sermons, "Rosary beads are not just for Hail Marys anymore."

I would suggest using the beads to say 'Faith' over and over again on the 59 beads. Or say 'Help' 59 times. Or 'Grace' or 'Peace' – or 'Lord, make me an instrument of your peace' 59 times – one for each bead.

I have often said, "Be creative. Ask the Lord to help these 59 people today." Then see if you can think of 59 people to pray for – one for each bead.

Nobody has criticized me for thinking outside the box.

I also like to say, "Here's a way to give a Jewish or non-Catholic friend a pair of Rosary beads as a gift. Here's a way to get others to pray."

Use the beads to come up with 59 things – 59 moments in your life – 59 people in your life you are thankful for.

Rosary beads are worry beads – or sleep-inducing beads. They are a great way to feel connected with all the people on the planet and with all the religions of the world. Amen.

Mere Christianity

If anyone wants the name of a great book on some of the topics I'm talking about in this book, they should buy a copy of *Mere Christianity* by C.S. Lewis.

It's a small book that actually comprises four books. It's the printed version of a series of talks by C.S. Lewis from the 1940s.

You can still purchase it at Barnes and Noble. I don't know how much the book costs now. It's listed for $2.95 on the paper back copy I have in my room.

When I was serving as a parish priest I would buy a copy of this book and go through it with people interested in the Catholic faith – even though it wasn't a Catholic book. It was simply a description of *Mere Christianity*.

After the preface, the table of contents provides an overview of what the book covers.

Book I – RIGHT AND WRONG AS A CLUE TO THE MEANING OF THE UNIVERSE

1. The Law of Human Nature
2. Some Objections
3. The Reality of the Law
4. What Lies Behind the Law
5. We Have Cause to Be Uneasy

7.   Let's Pretend
8.   Is Christianity Hard or Easy?
9.   Counting the Cost
10.   Nice People or New Men
11.   The New Men

Now that's a very good listing of topics this book covers. It also tells the reader some of the main issues to understand when trying to merely understand Christianity.

We need to do the same for Catholicism

Catholic
Noun or Adjective

The word 'catholic' can be both a noun and an adjective.

I learned this when I was reading the book, *Mere Christianity*. In that book C.S. Lewis, the author, says Christian can be both a noun or an adjective.

A Christian can be a good Christian or a bad Christian.

It can depend on whether they are living a Christian way of life or not.

There are practicing Catholics and non-practicing Catholics.

I could become a non-practicing Catholic. Then again, in case of an accident I might re-start doing some Catholic things.

C.S. Lewis uses the word 'gentleman' to explain his thoughts about nouns and adjectives.

In the Preface to his book on *Mere Christianity* he puts it this way. "The word gentleman originally meant something recognizable; one had a coat of arms and some landed property. When you called someone a 'gentleman' you were not paying a compliment, but merely stating a fact. If you said he was not 'a gentleman' you were not insulting him, but giving information."

Notice how clear his writing is.

He continues, "There was no contradiction in saying that John was a liar and a gentleman; any more that there now is in saying that James is a fool and a M.A."

Next he points out how language and customs change.

"But then there came people who said – so rightly, charitably, spiritually, sensitively, so anything but usefully – 'Ah, but surely the important thing about a gentleman is not the coat of arms and the land, but the behavior? Surely he is the true gentleman who behaves like a gentleman should? Surely in that sense Edward is far more truly a gentleman than John?' They meant well. To be honorable and courteous and brave is of course a far better thing than to have a coat of arms. But it is not the same thing. Worse still, it is not a thing everyone will agree about. To call a man 'a gentleman' in this new, refined sense, becomes, in fact, not a way of giving information about him, but a way of praising him: to deny that he is 'a gentleman' becomes simply a way of insulting him."

C.S. Lewis continues, "When a word ceases to be a term of description and becomes merely a term of praise, it no longer tells you facts about the object: it only tells you about the speaker's attitude to that object."

More: (A 'nice' meal only means a meal the speaker likes.) A gentleman. Once it has been spiritualized and refined out of its old coarse, objective sense, means hardly more than a man whom the speaker likes. As a result, gentleman is now a useless word. We had lots of terms of approval already, so it was not needed for that use; on the other hand if anyone (say, in a historical work) wants to use it in its old sense, he cannot do so without explanations, it has been spoiled for that purpose.

Notice how I broke down some of these long paragraphs of C.S. Lewis into shorter ones to try to make his points clearer about the word Christian or Catholic being used as a noun or an adjective.

Time and language changes.

While Driving

While driving to a funeral, I had a thought…

I often have thoughts while driving – alone or with one other person. Not with three or four, for some reason.

This time, I was with one other person, but I started talking to myself. "What happens to people who have given up on God, or the Church, or faith, and they are at a funeral or a wedding taking place in a church?"

"Do they wonder?"

"Do they ever want a second chance – this time in a church or synagogue?"

"Our marriage is going okay, but God stuff sneaks in."

Those thoughts, those questions triggered a memory.

I was at the wedding of a cousin's child. I didn't know the bride and groom, but they didn't want anything Irish, Jewish, or Catholic at their wedding. Nothing.

They had three readings at their wedding ceremony, I think. The second reading was from a poetry book – Saint Paul's description of what love is, from his First Letter to the Corinthians. I recognized it because it's a reading chosen for 78% of Catholic church weddings – and I've performed hundreds of weddings as a priest.

The priest sitting next to me – a close friend of my cousin – nudged me after that reading and whispered, "God sneaks in every time."

After the wedding ceremony, I struck up a conversation with this priest. I didn't know him. He told me that my cousin had confided in him about how difficult it was that her daughter and son-in-law didn't want anything Irish, Jewish, or religious at their wedding.

I asked him about his comment, "God sneaks in every time."

He said, "I found it interesting." He paused and then said, "In that section of First Corinthians – Chapter 13: 1 to 13 – there are many mentions of love, but no mention of God. Whoever added this Bible text to the poetry book – added God in."

Then he smiled and said again, "God sneaks in every time."

That marriage – unfortunately – didn't last.

I didn't know that priest. My sister called me to tell me a heartbreaking story around the time of September 11th. She said, "That priest who was sitting next to you at our cousin's child's wedding was Father Mychal Judge."

He was the first recorded fatality of the September 11, 2001 attack on the World Trade Center in Manhattan, New York City.

What do people think about at funerals and weddings?

What about someone – anyone – who's at a church funeral or wedding? They are sitting there, experiencing a profoundly religious ceremony. The priest knows the deceased or the couple getting married. Everything feels so personal.

They see stained glass windows. They ponder the Stations of the Cross lining both sides of the church – 14 images. They listen to a beautiful rendition of the Ave Maria. They observe a statue of Christ with outstretched arms above the high altar.

Parents often ask priests about their children not going to church, or not having their grandchildren baptized.

Then comes a question I've heard a thousand times in recent years: "What will they do when they face tough times?"

Sometimes they add, "Okay, counseling could help… but what about God? What about God when times get tough?"

Sometimes I share the Mychal Judge quote: "God sneaks in every time." Sometimes I don't know what to say.

What Are Your Questions?

In the early 1970s, we used to say morning Mass down the road from where I was living on the New Jersey shore – at a retreat house named *Stella Maris* – Latin for Star of the Sea.

An interesting former professor – retired – Clement Jedrzejewski – of St. Francis College in Brooklyn, N.Y. got a room there – in this nun's retreat house. I noticed he didn't have a car – so I said to him once, "If you ever need to get to a barber or the mall or wherever, let me know."

I got to know him a bit as a result. He had taught educational methodology at St. Francis. So on one trip to the mall, I told him I helped with about 10 high school retreats a year. I then asked: any suggestions?

He asked me a few questions. Then he said, "Let me think about this – then on some future trip – we can talk about this."

About a month later, he said, "First step: get people's questions."

His mantra was: "There are no stupid questions – only stupid answers."

Then he said, "Can I see your retreat house?"

Like Stella Maris – just down the road – it too was on the Atlantic Ocean.

He asked how the kids got there and where they were from.

He said, "When they get off the bus – let them unwind – and walk around."

He added, "When a dog comes into a house or a new place – he likes to walk around – and sniff around. So let the young people coming on retreat sniff around the whole place. Then you can begin the retreat."

"Get the young people's questions."

Once more tell them, "There are no stupid questions – only stupid answers."

"Get them to write down on paper all their questions – about their lives – about their parents – about their school?"

He said, "Tell them there will be more questions."
Then he said, "Tell them to look at your questions and pick out three that stand out. Put a circle around them or whatever."

Then he said, "Tell them to put that paper or papers in their pocket."

"Next," he said. "Pick out someone in the room – just one person – whom you think you can talk to."

"Then," he said, "Find a good place to talk with that person – inside or outside. Once more jot down all your questions. Some will be the same as the questions in your pocket – some will be different."

"Then pick out the three most important questions."

"Then," he said, "One of you pocket them."

"Next," he said, "Pick out a small group – four or five – people you can talk to. Pick people you know – people whom you will be with and talk with – at times – after you get home."

"Then jot down all the questions you have – about the school – about the retreat – about God – about friends – about your future."

"Tell them, several times; there are no stupid questions – only stupid answers."

"Give them those large pieces of white paper – and list on that paper – three questions – they would like to look at during this retreat."

"Then hang them on the walls of the conference room. Then at a big session – have them walk around the room – and read the white papers."

"Then," he said, "have the whole group talk about the questions they have in their pockets – or questions they shared one-to-one – or in small groups – and now the ones on the walls."

"Then," he said, "say, finally after this exhausting exercise, pick the three top questions you would like to talk about for the three days we're here on retreat."

It worked. It was tricky. We got into discussions about relationships, cliques, not knowing each other, college, what we want to do with our lives, and family. Sometimes we got into religion – but usually not.

Looking back, I think the biggest learning was, "We have lots of questions, and none of them are stupid."

I ended up using that method in counseling. I kept in mind something I have heard psychologists saying, "Remember! The presenting problem is never the problem."

Ask questions: "Is there any other worry you have?" "Have you talked to other people about this?" "What came up?" "If someone came to you with this question, what would you ask about?"

Ask people: "What about this book? What are you expecting? Did anything hit you yet? What's missing?"

Twenty Questions

In this book, I am asking and attempting to provoke questions, particularly about religion and being a Catholic.

Try to generate twenty thought-provoking questions. Use a computer or pen and paper to write them down. Discuss your questions with others and ask for their thoughts. Encourage them to provide their own list of twenty questions, and if they feel comfortable, some answers as well.

As time passes, examine your questions and make improvements. Learn from them.

Here are twenty questions that I find interesting:

1) What's the best question you have ever been asked?
2) Have you ever had a religious experience? Describe what happened.
3) Name a movie that moved you? Describe why?
4) Best book you ever read? Describe the whys?
5) If you wrote your life, your autobiography, what would be its title?

6) What would be the chapters of your autobiography?

7) Best Catholic you ever met? Please fill that one out?

8) Rate yourself as a Catholic – 10 being the highest rating?

9) If you could become a priest, would you go for it?

10) If you could preach one sermon, what would be its message?

11) Do you believe in God?

12) Best teacher you ever had?

13) Your favorite song or hymn?

14) Best day of my life so far?

15) What I'd want my legacy to be?

16) The most significant moment in my life so far?

17) Best meal I ever had?

18) When I was most angry?

19) Whom do I love? Describe.

20) When did I feel most alone? Describe.

There Are Other Restaurants in Town

We all know folks who have dropped out of church – who have stopped going to Mass.

They complain about monotone mumblers in the pulpit or preachers who only talk about money, money, money.

I heard a priest – after hearing another priest talk about nieces and nephews not going to church – because of boring, boring services – saying, "There are other restaurants in town."

Now that makes sense – but it better be a better restaurant.

It doesn't when we sense there's another reason – not being voiced.

Sometimes someone is simply looking for a reason to jump ship or to get on a different train.

Sunday mass just doesn't have a grab. Guilt has disappeared. There are better things to do on a Sunday morning than go to church. Sleep in if you've been out late on a Saturday night. That feels much better. So, bye bye, American pie…drive your Chevy to a levee for a better use of your time.

So there are better restaurants in town…

People miss out on great movies – great books – or great meals.

At baptisms or weddings or funerals I notice faces off to the side. I watch. I wonder. I ask myself what's going on in their brains.

Does anyone ever get the thought: "What's going on here?"

Maybe there is a God and God is on this Merry-Go-Round and I'm not on it.

God, do you ever go fishing – like for ME?

Women Priests
in the Catholic Church

In our parish we had a nice custom of giving new altar servers a 'Shout Out' when they served Mass for the first time.

It was always on a Sunday – it was when their family was there.

Scott – who trained the altar servers – would come over to me – before the Mass – if I was the priest at that Mass – and introduce me to the kid or kids – who were about to be altar servers for the first time.

I'd say, "Congratulations. Thanks. And relax!"

Then after Communion – just before the final prayers and the final blessing – I would say something like this to the folks at that Mass, "We had two new altar servers today – serving for the first time – Jake and Patricia. Congratulations. Thank you. Let's give them a hand."

And everyone would clap!

Well, this one Sunday morning we had one brand new server: Mary.

That last week we had just got a new pope, so without much thinking, I connected the two. I said something like this. It was not prepared. "We got a new pope last week and we got a new altar server this Sunday morning, Mary."

Then I added, "And Mary, who knows, if you end up a great server, some day you might be made pope."

Laughter and clapping.

After Mass – after I had said, "Good bye" to the folks – a lady came over to me and said, "How could you have said what you said?"

I said, "Said what?"

She said, "You're for women priests!"

I said, "When did I say that?"

"You said that Mary, the server today, could someday be made pope."

I paused. I thought. I finally got what she was saying. I said, "You gotta get a sense of humor."

I could see she was still furious. She walked away.

That afternoon I got a phone call from that lady asking for an appointment to see me around 3:30 – with her husband.

I said, "Gladly."

They arrived at 3:30 – with a gigantic blue-covered book. I think it was blue and it must have had 763 pages. One of those books…

Her husband remained quiet – but she told me this was a book by a German theologian. She said it says there cannot ever be women priests.

I remained quiet.

Finally, I said, "I wasn't pushing women priests. I was just giving this little girl named Mary a shout out."

"But," I butted in with a comment. "By the year 55,000 do you mean to say, 'We will not have women priests in the Catholic Church?'"

She said, "We won't. Guaranteed."

I said, "I wasn't pushing women priests – but when we're in heaven together – look me up – if they have women priests."

I was tempted to say, "If and when we have women priests," but why ruin a perfectly nice Sunday afternoon? And my football Giants were on TV.

You Didn't Tell Me
She Was Catholic

Everyone – by now – has heard the joke about the lady whose cat died.

So she had the thought, I wonder if I could have a funeral Mass for my cat, Daisy.

She went to her church – dropped into the rectory – and asked to see her priest. She was crying – and tearfully made her request for a funeral Mass for her cat. He said, "Sorry. I just can't do that."

Seeing her tears flowing even more – after his 'No. Sorry', he tried to recover by adding, "There's a Protestant Church just up the street from here. Maybe they could do a nice service for Dotty."

"Her name is Daisy, Father. Her name is Daisy."

Then the lady said, "Father, one more question. Do you think $5,000 is enough to give to that Protestant Church if they will do a service?"

The priest said, "Wait a minute now. You didn't tell me that Daisy was a Catholic?"

That joke always gets a laugh. It does. It doesn't have too much of an edge in it. I notice priests always laugh with and at it – even if they have heard variations of that joke 100 times.

It's pretty much the same joke about the Mafia guy who came to the parish church for his brother's funeral. "Father I'll make a $10,000 gift extra – if you say in your sermon – that my brother was a saint. That would really mean a lot to his family."

The priest paused for a moment. Then he said, "I can do that."

At the funeral – during the sermon – the priest slipped in the following short comment: "Compared to his brother, he was a saint."

That comment got a cute laugh – as well as the $10,000 check.

The Catholic Church has its saints as well as its sinners.

Catholics have their stories – sometimes sad stories – about times they heard the word 'No' from the Church,

There's a story about the aunt who was told by some priest she couldn't receive communion because she got divorced and remarried – but didn't get an annulment.

Then sometimes someone adds, "I heard of some priest who said in a similar situation, 'You can't kick people out of the family – ever. And you don't invite people to come to your home and then say, you can't eat anything.'"

Tricky stuff. Tricky stuff.

Hopefully people can get annulments from their marriages. Hopefully people can get counseling when a marriage falls apart. Hopefully priests and deacons and parishes can be helpful when people have their troubles.

Hopefully priests who don't like pets, respect those who do. Hopefully they have on or around October 4, the feast of St. Francis of Assisi, or a similar feast, the Blessing of the Animals.

Human beings, Catholics or Atheists, or whoever, need to have great respect for each other. Amen.

To Be or Not to
Be a Catholic
When I Am a Catholic?

To be or not to be a Catholic when I am a Catholic?

That's a basic question this book is asking.

It seems that lots of folks have stopped going to Church. That's an 'Uh oh' if you're a Catholic priest.

We've always had Christmas and Easter Catholics – but when asked about their religion, would say, "Oh, I'm a Catholic."

Now it seems to me: a new nuance has arisen. People have announced, "Oh, I'm no longer a Catholic."

I'm wondering how much thought has gone into their decision – if that is what they are doing.

Was it a voiced opinion – and decision?

Did they just stop going to Church – as a signal to themselves – and to some others: "I am no longer a Catholic?"

I know one person who stopped going to Church – because they were sick and tired of the preacher's sermons – who was constantly harping on gays. "Enough already."

He felt, he didn't have a vote.

He felt, he didn't have a voice.

He felt, he didn't have a chance to receive "Good News: the Good News of Jesus Christ at a Sunday Mass."

I'd be stupid as priest to challenge him – by saying, "There's other parts of the Mass – the prayers, the worship, the acknowledging of God, being with a community of believers, receiving Holy Communion, joining in the services of that community, helping with a Food Pantry, helping once a year with housing, being a religious ed. teacher, helping on an auction committee – as a parish fund raiser."

I would say what I say in this book: "Like restaurants, there are other churches in the area."

If I had time I might ask, "Did you see the movie *Brooklyn*?" Then if they did I'd ask what they thought of the priest in it – Father Flood – and the Parish Community Ellis Lacey (Saoirse Ronan) belonged to?

I'd ask – if I could ask questions: "Have you ever been in a great parish? Have you ever met a wonderful priest or nun? Have you ever read a great religious book? Have you ever made a religious workshop? Have you ever tried other religious communities?"

I would listen.

I'd ask follow up questions.

I'd ask if they went to Catholic Schools – and what is their take on that experience.

If I met them in an office at a Catholic Church, as background, I'd want to have several bookcases of Catholic books. I would point out books like, *The Confessions of Augustine.*

I would want them to have the big picture.

I would want to say that the Catholic Church has been around for 2000 years.

I'd use time lines – history lines. For example I would talk a bit about Early Church persons, the Protestant Reformation, Catholics and the Bible.

By dropping out of the Catholic Church, I'd want them to realize they are giving up a lot more than not hearing a complaining priest.

By talking to another, they might hear what they are talking to themselves about. People often do some significant re-thinking – that night or the next day after an emotional complaint session.

I'd talk about visiting Catholic churches – to look around – in any city they are visiting. I'd mention Notre Dame in Paris and St. Patrick's Cathedral in New York City.

I would tell them to pray – to have a spot you love – in some chapel or church – and go there in the quiet in the late afternoon.

I would add: "Have a prayer chair in your house and a quiet time to pray."

Have a prayer book – and collect 7 good prayers – to put in that prayer book – plus death cards for that prayer book – and call it your private cemetery.

I'd ask them to do research and have conversations with family members on how long have they been Catholic – and what were the churches the family attended – and visit those churches and talk to their ancestors about their faith journey.

Do different!

Habitus Non Facit Monachum

There is an old Latin phrase, *"Habitus non facit monachum."*

A habit – a cassock – a robe – does not make the monk.

The rosary does not make the Catholic.

The uniform does not make the soldier or the cop.

Well, then, what makes a Catholic? What makes a Christian?

As I said earlier on in this book, C. S. Lewis would say Baptism makes the Christian. Then one lives one's life hopefully as a good Christian.

He said that it would be the same for a gentleman. That's a title. It means this person has some land. Hopefully he'll be a good gentleman and a good neighbor and a good person.

So too a Catholic. Catholic is a noun signifying a person has been baptized and follows the creed and the descriptions of a Catholic in a Catechism.

That seems to be a smart way to state this. We can attend a Baptism. We can see the water being poured on a person's head. We can hear the words of baptism, "I baptize you _______________ (Name) in the name of the Father, and the Son and the Holy Spirit. Amen. Amen."

Certificates, licenses, diplomas, degrees are part of life.

If we need a dentist or a doctor, we want to know they have the credentials and the training.

If the rule in the Catholic Church is: if you want to marry a Catholic. The Catholic party must bring in a document that states when and where they were baptized. Each church has these big books that list the baptized.

Do you have a Baptismal certificate? It's important to have one in your files.

Catholic Church Ushers

In the Catholic Church, there is no Hall of Fame for ushers.

In Catholic parishes in the United States, there are many ushers who are great servants. Up until 1960, most were males, but if you travel around and stop in for Mass at different parishes, you'll spot women doing the job.

Growing up in Brooklyn in the 1950s or so, most ushers at movies were women.

I think it was in St. Louis or near there that they had a great usher who had Down Syndrome. This was around 1970.

Tommy's dream was to be an usher.

He nagged and nagged, asked and asked, but his pastor and parish didn't have the imagination to give Tommy a chance to be an usher.

He didn't give up, and at the age of 24, Tommy got his chance.

Lesson #1 was the job to stand there in the back of the church and welcome everyone in with that one word, "Welcome," with a smile.

Tommy had that gift, and everyone got his smile as he pointed to possible seats or led folks to seats he just knew they would like. He knew where the 11 possible places in the church for people in wheelchairs and walkers were.

But that wasn't enough. That kind of ushering was easy.

A whole new world opened when Mack, the head usher, asked Tommy if he thought he could collect the collection.

This was the moment Tommy was waiting for.

The first month went perfectly.

At money collecting time, Tommy marched down the main aisle, the left side of the church, and reached into each bench with the hard straw basket on long poles. People put in their envelopes, cash, checks.

Surprise. Surprise. If a 'customer' didn't put anything into the collection basket, Tommy would go 'Uuuumf, Uuumph' and gesture, sort of pushing the basket into that person, until they reached for their wallet and put some cash into the basket. Tommy was sort of loud and sort of persistent.

The parishioners of that parish had never seen such a scene before. They loved it. Tommy got those cheapskates to do their duty.

Mack, the head usher, heard about it and said, "Uh oh! What did we do?"

But when he heard the funny part of the story, he too loved it.

The collection went up about $300 a week. And the pastor loved it.

Tommy was in, and the word went around the diocese. "You should drop into Our Lady of Hope Church next Sunday. They have this great usher who has doubled the Sunday collection."

Exaggerations make stories that much better, every time.

Saints: Google Them

There are many saints in the Catholic Church. Google them.

Here's a list of some of them: Google them. At the local library – and/or if you have a parish library, look around to see if they have something like Butler's Lives of the Saints.

Pick one saint at a time. Read two or three short listings or descriptions of the same saint and compare, compare, compare.

Here's a starting list of some saints to google or to look up:

Saint Augustine
Saint Agnes
Saint Bernard
Saint Monica,
Saint Philip Neri,
Saint Catherine of Siena
Saint Athanasius,
Saint Gregory the Great,
Saint Vincent de Paul,
Saint Martin de Porres,
Saint Nicholas

Saint Andrew Avellino

Saint Thomas Becket,

St. Elizabeth of Hungary

Saint Cecilia,

St. Martin of Tours

St. John of the Cross

St. Peter Canisius

St. Teresa of the Child Jesus

St. Dominic

St. John the Baptist

St. Blasé

St. Francis de Sales.

Saint Francis of Assisi

Saint Francis Xavier

Kind of Catholics

Jack and Jill went up the hill – to their church – every Sunday of their lives – just to get a pail of water. Sometimes they got their fill; sometimes they went home empty.

That is, that is till they moved down south after their retirement. That is, till they found themselves in a great parish in the middle of nowhere.

For the next 4 years, they began telling their friends on the phone back north how lucky they were to find the church they found.

It was not their plan to look at churches when it came to the place they wanted to move to. Weather and being relatively close to where their kids lived – kids with kids – that's what they wanted. "We wanted to see our grandkids – that's what we really wanted."

So they moved. They got a good price on their house up north. They got a nice house down south by the water. But the big surprise was the parish they ended up in. Surprise. Surprise. Surprise. It was so good, but it wasn't in their plans.

The second Sunday there, they noticed mention on a bulletin board in the vestibule: "Parish Picnic – Sunday afternoon – 2 till 5 – August 16 – Wear your T-shirt."

They asked, "T-shirt?"

They got answers like, "You'll see?" – "You haven't heard about our T-shirts?"

"Surprise. Surprise. You'll be wearing yours next year. Guaranteed."

"Bring your own chair."

They got there that Sunday afternoon at 1:30 – early – great weather – perfect day – lots of people with tables and cooking grills and smoke. Lots of smoke.

Everybody had their T-shirts on. They started to read them. There were 10 different types of Catholics – in 10 different circles – but today mixed up.

Matthew 25 Visiting Catholics

Luke 15 Family Forgiveness Catholics.

Luke 10: 25–37 Good Samaritan Catholics

John 6 Eucharistic Catholics.

Luke 17: 11–19 Thank You Catholics.

Luke 18:15–17 Kid Catholics.

Luke 10: 38–42 Martha – Mary Catholics.

Mark 12: 28–34 Greatest Commandment Catholics.

1st Corinthians 13: 4–3 Catholics.

Galatians 6:3 Catholics.

That was 10 groups – 10 small communities – within the larger community.

To start a new group you had to have at least 12 members. You had to have a biblical text – a one-liner that all agreed upon – and you had to make a commitment to that group for at least a year.

There was no problem switching to another group after a year. The thinking for that was to promote new views – new behaviors – new ways of being a Catholic.

Meetings were monthly – and you had to make at least 6 a year.

Oh yeah, and you had to get a T-shirt – any color – with the title of your group on the back.

The idea surfaced a good thirty years ago when Catholics started moving to the south more and more. They found out that Protestants thought Catholics never used or read the Bible.

Surprise! Surprise! Read our T-shirts.

The Matthew 25 Catholics – actually it was Matthew 25: 31–46…they were the doers – the ones who visited the sick, the old, the imprisoned, getting food to the hungry and drink to the thirsty, the ones who welcomed the strangers.

That was important for every Catholic to do those things for those who needed help.

So too Galatians 6:3 Catholics. Those who got this message and this T-shirt and this nuance felt they finally had the secret of following Christ. Bearing each other's burdens…lifting each other's burdens…it was such a clear message. If your grandmother had one of these type persons on her street – you knew she would never get a bad back.

Mark 12 Catholics…it took a while to grasp their message. It was the great commandment: Mark 12: 28–34. They would tell each other how they had to grasp the secrets of the key words in the Great Commandment. It takes good time to learn how to love with our whole heart, soul, mind and strength. Then we have to learn to love our neighbor as we love ourselves – and to do all this with balance and completeness.

Luke 17 was about the 'Thank You Catholics'. They believed that one needed to spend at least a whole year practicing gratitude. All they had to do was take a few moments each day to say the two powerful words, "Thank you!" People in town and within families could easily identify when they were living or interacting with a Thank You Catholic.

Luke 10 featured the Martha Mary Catholics. This group was the most distinctive of all. They typically consisted of two women, such as sisters or mother-daughter pairs, but not always. It was especially fascinating when they embodied both Martha and Mary qualities, although that was a rare occurrence. Nevertheless, outsiders loved to inquire, "Who is the Martha, and who is the Mary?"

Luke 15 showcased the families who recognized the importance of practicing forgiveness for the sake of their unity. Every family that experienced a significant rupture needed to invest time and love into the healing process. It required a lot of effort, therapy, prayer, and attentive listening to facilitate healing.

Luke 10:25–37 introduced the Good Samaritan Catholics. They understood the significance of stopping and offering help. They acknowledged that every person on the streets before them was a brother or sister in need, deserving of their assistance.

John 6 focused on the Eucharist Catholics. They deeply appreciated the act of consuming the bread of life, which symbolized Christ. They believed that this daily practice was essential for gaining eternal life.

Luke 18:15–17 reminded us not to forget the gift of embracing our inner child. We should express our sense of humor, enjoy playfulness, engage in games, laughter, singing, and cherish the company of others through activities such as card games, Monopoly, or puzzles.

1st Corinthians 13:4–13 highlighted the love-centered Catholics. They strived to be patient, understanding, and kind to one another every day.

Similar initiatives were attempted in various parts of the United States, and there were reports of a parish in Canada practicing this program. However, in general, the parish in the southern region was considered the most successful in implementing this unique approach.

By the way, out of these ten groups, which one would you choose to join initially?

A First for Me

A president once made some nasty comments about people's homes – in Haiti, in Africa as well as in the United States.

I received a few phone calls from parishioners who said, "You have to say something about this."

So I did.

It was a first for me.

I realized some people might think I'm bringing politics into the pulpit.

I said in my sermon at the 8:30 Sunday morning Mass, "We have Redemptorists in Haiti and one of the priests in our house here is from Zimbabwe." Then I added, "I think it's immoral to make fun of the homes of other human beings."

At the end of the homily, everyone clapped.

I found out later that not everybody clapped. Some people walked out.

I preached the same message again that morning at the Sunday 11 AM Mass. I wasn't doing it for the clap – but because I thought it was right – and that our Church has standards and values. Once more the full church clapped and this time some stood and clapped.

I felt funny. This was a first for me – in being a priest for over 50 years.

At the end of every Sunday Mass we walk down the aisle and head for the vestibule at the entrance to the church. We wish everyone a 'Hello' and 'Have a great week'.

After that Mass about 25 people came at me – yelling comments like, "You're for abortion!"

"I came here for Mass – not politics."

Oooh, I thought. *Uh oh!*

Then another group who were at that Mass came over to support me!

A physical fight didn't happen.

Letters and phone calls did happen. They were mostly critical – that Sunday and Monday.

One man wrote,

I'm out of this Church. You won't get any more checks from me.

If a letter had an address of a phone number, I contacted that person.

I invited them in to talk or I would go to their house.

I did see about three persons in person.

This was the first time anything like this had ever happened to me. It made me think a lot more than any other sermon I had ever preached. I remembered hearing, "If people never want to crucify you, maybe you're not preaching the messages of Jesus Christ. Maybe you don't know what it means to be a prophet. Jeremiah was thrown down a pit for preaching justice."

I know that preaching is not about me or about politics or about money. I know the gospel is about treating people, their families, and their homes with respect, love, and dignity.

Mary

If there is one thing that Catholics are known for all around the world, it's this: Mary, the mother of Jesus – the Blessed Virgin Mary – the Mother of God – is part of their lives.

Non-Catholics often don't understand how Catholics see Mary as part of our lives.

They might grasp Mary as an example on how to live life to the fullest, but they don't understand Mary as someone we pray to.

They think we see her as God. No, we don't. She isn't God. But that's how some people perceive Catholics.

Go into Catholic churches all around the world – and you will find images, pictures, and statues of Mary everywhere. Churches are named after her. Prayers are said to her. Songs are sung to her.

In the Gospel of John, there is an early story about Jesus being invited to a wedding with his mother. There must have been a lot of people who showed up at this wedding – because they ran out of wine.

The word was out that Jesus can solve any problem, so those with the wine problem go to Mary who says to go to Jesus and "Do whatever he tells you."

He says, "It's not my time!"

It's a good storytelling. He solves the problem and he changes water into wine – lots of wine – 12 gigantic water jars become wine.

Jesus does it – but the key message in the story is to go to Mary and she'll tell you to do whatever Jesus tells you to do.

And that's the key to all the stories about Mary and Jesus.

Go to Mary and she'll tell you to do whatever Jesus tells you to do.

Lourdes

In September of 1955 – our 3rd year of high school – Father John Barry, whom we had for Latin, told us, "If you ever get the chance to go to Lourdes in France, go."

He added, "And if you go, go to the baths there!"

In 1996, four of us went to Lourdes. We were my brother-in-law, my two sisters, and I. We spent one week in Ireland – where our parents were from – in County Galway. Then we took a ferry from Cobb on the east coast of Ireland to Le Havre in France. We then took a train from there to Paris. Then we caught a train south to Lourdes.

We got a hotel room, then had some supper, and then we went to one of the biggest shrines to Mary in the world: Lourdes.

It had people, people from everywhere. We marched in a procession, said the rosary with the crowd, and got the time schedule for the next day.

Then we went back to the hotel and got the sleep we needed.

We were spending a week in France after a week in Ireland. Each of us had the pick of a place. My brother-in-law, Jerry, picked Paris. My sister Peggy, the nun, picked Lourdes, a lifetime dream. My sister Mary picked Bordeaux, and I picked Chartres.

For the procession that second night in Lourdes, my sister Peggy bought 4 candles – but got the wrong candles. She had to rip the cardboard from her pantyhose stocking holders – to make holders for our candles. Besides the crowds, the ceremonies, the large contingents of folks in wheelchairs, and the baths, I remember the candles in the cardboard pantyhose containers.

We went to the baths in the afternoon. I remembered loud and clear the urgent message from Father John Barry to make sure we did that.

My 2 sisters wouldn't do it. My brother-in-law Jerry and I went to the men's lockers, stripped, got wrapped in a big towel, and went to the big bathtubs. Attendants took our towels and one by one we were dunked totally in the big tubs. Some words in French – probably some prayers – were said over us when we were in the water. We were taken out – covered by the big white towels – and brought back to our lockers to get our clothes back on.

Everyone who has gone to the Lourdes baths praised the moment as a life blessing. I felt bad I failed to convince my 2 sisters to get in the baths. My brother-in-law was forever thankful that I told him to go for it.

Lourdes – go for it.

Lourdes – read anything you can get on the story of that shrine and on the life of Bernadette of Lourdes.

Bernadette Soubirous was born in 1844. She had serious health problems while growing up. She was poor and poorly educated, but had amazing apparitions in February of 1858.

Bernadette experienced major opposition, yet a chapel was built in 1862. By the end of the Franco-Prussian War of 1870, Lourdes was major. But Bernadette was not. She did not play up her experience. She kept quiet – unless directly asked. She had health problems even though people were going to Lourdes for healings. In 1864, she tried to enter the Sisters of Notre Dame of Nevers, but was kept back for health reasons until 1866. That was her life – a nun there until her death on April 16, 1879.

Miracle stories were told about her, but they were made up. The apparition stories were the major stories and that was it. Yet she was canonized a saint by 1933 because of her life of prayer and balance.

As someone described her: "She was an ordinary visionary if ever there was one – and that was it." Yet Lourdes became extraordinary. Go there and go to the baths. You will never regret or forget the experience.

Chartres Cathedral

I once spotted an old black vinyl round record by Charles Laughton. He read some stories and told about his experiences of going to Chartres Cathedral when he was 19 years of age.

Sort of by accident…and sort of by accident – while at Chartres – he got a guided tour by Etienne Houvet. He ended up staying three days and experienced a lot more.

Charles Laughton experienced the most famous shrine in France of Mary, the mother of Jesus: Chartres Cathedral. He spotted a guide and asked if a certain window was from the 12th or 13th century. That question led to everything.

25 years later he goes to Paris again – while making the movie, *The Hunchback of Notre Dame*. He decides to go to Chartres again and once more meets Etienne Houvet. Laughton is asked, "How did you do?"

He told Etienne he did fine and once more got the tour.

Years later he became friends with the modern artist Manessier who invites him to France to see a whole series of his new paintings. While there he tells Manessier that he's going to Chartres after seeing him. Manessier asks, "Can I go with you?"

Laughton says, "Gladly!" He thought it would be a great experience seeing Chartres with a great artist. It wasn't that far away. While driving, while talking, both became very quiet.

Then the question: "You met him too?"

Both had met Etienne Houvet, the great tour guide of Chartres. When they got there, they compared notes. It was one more highlight of the life of Charles Laughton.

He found out that this artist – like this cathedral – had the purpose to show us humans what it's like to be chased by God. Stained glass windows, brick, color, and art can bring us to God.

After listening to that record, that story by Charles Laughton, it became my hope to someday get to Chartres.

I'm talking to a priest friend of mine who told me that while studying in Paris he once went to Chartres. I said, "You have to listen to this record of mine – that tells all about Charles Laughton's trip to Chartres."

We both listened to the talk on the record that I had by Laughton. When over, he tells me, "Guess what?" He then tells me when he was there he got the Chartres tour by Etienne Houvet's daughter.

A month after this my sister Mary told me there was an article in the Sunday magazine of the Philadelphia Inquirer about Malcolm Miller the famous tour guide of Chartres.

It was all coming together for me. A few months later my two sisters, my brother-in-law, and I got off the train in Chartres, and walked to the Cathedral and received the morning and afternoon tours by Malcolm Miller.

Visiting Great Catholic Churches

To be a Catholic is to feel at home in any Catholic Church in the world.

It's the opposite of how one feels when entering a synagogue or a Mormon temple. We know when we are in a different religious place and when we feel at home.

I was fortunate to hear about and visit not only Lourdes and Chartres, but also several other great Catholic Churches in the world.

There are more to come.

In 1995, after spending two weeks with my two sisters and my brother-in-law in Ireland and France, I took another week by myself and went to Hamburg, Germany. On my way back by train to Paris and the airport to return to the United States, my niece's husband at the time advised me to take an earlier train. He told me to get off the train in Cologne and see the great cathedral there. "It's only a street away from the train station."

I did it, even though I didn't have a reserved seat on the train from Hamburg to Cologne. There was a Mass taking place. I saw the church and the big clock across the street. It was well worth it. I only truly appreciate the value of my decisions after I make them. And then, on the train, I got the seat I had originally purchased to travel from Hamburg to Paris.

The next major church on my bucket list was Sagrada Familia in Barcelona, Spain. I have been there twice and would go again and again if I could.

It was supposed to be completed by 2026, the centennial year of Antoni Gaudi's death. However, the COVID-19 pandemic caused delays. Will I still be alive by the time it's finished?

Much of the money for the construction came from private donations by visitors, amounting to around 2 million per year.

Construction began in 1882, with Francisco de Paula del Villar in charge, but he resigned in 1883.

That's when Antoni Gaudi took over, and Sagrada Familia became synonymous with his name.

I visited Sagrada Familia for the first time in 2009. We spent about three hours exploring the columns, lights, artwork, and unique beauty of the place. On my way out, I noticed a sign for the museum.

I asked the four people I was with if they were interested in the museum, but they weren't. We were on a cruise and only had a day to explore the city. I love museums, so I went and read all the information and history I could find.

For example, Gaudi incorporated the roots of trees at the base of the church's columns and pillars. I didn't notice them the first time I walked around the church.

I made a mental note and returned for a second tour of the church.

A couple of years later, on another cruise, I took a new tour of Sagrada Familia.

I want to go again when it's finally completed.

If you use the internet, search for 'Sagrada Familia' on YouTube or any other search engine and watch at least five short videos.

I guarantee that if you watch YouTube videos, you will see what you're missing. You will then visit Sagrada Familia when you have the opportunity.

Admitting It

Say it, if you are one, "I am a Catholic."

There I said it.

I admit it.

It's an 'I am'.

As I mention in this book, we have a few of these 'I ams'.

I am a Brooklynite.

I am of Irish background. Both my parents were born in Ireland before they came to America.

I am an American.

I am a Catholic priest.

I am a member of a religious congregation called 'The Redemptorists'.

I am a Los Angeles Dodger's fan. That's baseball.

I root for the New York Knicks when it comes to basketball – the New York Rangers when it comes to hockey – and the New York Giants when it comes to football.

Any of those allegiances to sporting teams could be shallow, superficial, or significant.

To say "I am a Catholic" can also be quite profound or rather superficial.

I like to say "I am a Christian."

But in this book I'm looking at the 'I am a Catholic' statement.

The Catholic bishops of the United States meet on a regular basis.

I would think they ought to consider "What's it like to be a Catholic?" I would assume it's much more than being against abortion.

Could they come up with a program that addresses the "What's it like to be a Catholic" question.

What would it be like to try a pilot program? For example to have a parish have 5 evenings of 2 hour sessions – on 5 answers – to the, "What is a Catholic?" question.

Five possible areas could be:

1) The History of the Catholic Church;
2) The Mystery of the Catholic Church;
3) The Creeds of the Catholic Church;
4) The Local Parish or Community;
5) The Future of the Catholic Church.

Videos, books, catechisms, group discussions, question and answer sessions, visiting a nursing home, etc. should be considered.

This would be centered on Adult Education. This would be centered on bringing it home for discussion. This would be Bible-centered.

I could see participants being given a button to wear that said, "I Am A Catholic" – after they finish the week-long program. They would be told they have a choice to wear that button – or make it a bumper sticker – or whatever they prefer.

Then they would be commissioned to recruit folks for the next time this program is offered – and so on.

My bottom line is simply to ask, "When you give up being a Catholic, do you realize what you're giving up – the Church's height and depth, its history and its mystery, the experience of life in Christ and with his body."

One Small Card

Somewhere along the line, someone gave me a small card with a message on it.

I keep that small card – 2 by 1 inch – in my priest prayer book. It's covered with see through plastic. I look at that card once a day – and connect with its sentiments.

It has more prayer energy than all the different psalms and short scripture readings in my prayer book.

I'm acknowledging God.

> *EACH*
>
> *DAY*
>
> *AT LEAST*
>
> *ONCE*
>
> *RETURN*
>
> *THE*
>
> *GAZE*
>
> *OF GOD.*
>
> *RICHARD ROHR*

The more I looked at this card in the past few years, the more I felt God acknowledging me.

Religious people acknowledge God.

I'm not alone.

Catholics acknowledge God.

While watching a baseball game on TV, I have often seen athletes point to the skies – point to God – when they get a key hit.

I can hear them thinking in that moment, "Not to us O Lord, but to your name, I give the glory."

One key purpose of this book is to get folks back to Church – because I would think Church goers – pray and acknowledge God more.

If you have dropped out of Church, have you dropped God out of your life?

Is the only time you acknowledge God,

the only time you return the gaze of God, when you have an accident – or when something spectacular happens and you say the automatic "Oh my God!"

7 Popes

Who have been the great popes?

Who have been the popes in our lifetime?

To be a Catholic is to have a pope – and to know about popes.

I have had 7 popes in my lifetime – so far.

I know more about them than any of the other popes – and there have been many – 200 plus.

Looking at them – how they acted and reacted to what was going on in our world – and looking up what happened in their lifetime can give anyone a wide-angle picture of what it is to be a Catholic.

For example, 3 of the 7 popes of my lifetime were named Time magazine's *Man or Person of the Year*: John XXIII (1963), John Paul II (1994), and Francis I (2013). Is there any chance I could find those lives online and read those magazine articles?

Each was part of a specific family as well as part of our world. What does their last names or family name – Pacelli, Roncalli, Montini, Wojtyla, Luciani, Ratzinger, and Bergoglio – trigger?

All were from Europe – except the present pope, Jorge Mario Bergoglio – who was from Argentina. Now that's a change of pace. Where will the next pope be from: North America, South America, Central America. Africa, Asia, or Europe?

In recent times there have been TV programs featuring some pretty bad popes: the Borgias for example. The ones I've seen have been good.

We have also seen several Popes declared Saints – so a title for a book about our different popes could be: *Saints and Sinners*.

Let me try to give a brief description of these 7 popes. It's part of being a Catholic to know one's pope.

Pope Pius XII

If interested in the life of Pius XII, I would suggest start by reading the Wikipedia document on him in the Internet. It's long: 19,494 words. Then there are 400 plus footnotes.

If you want to get into the life of Pius XII read *The Life and Pontificate of Pope Pius XII – Between History and Controversy* by Frank Coppa.

Or *The Pope at War: The Secret History of Pius XII, Mussolini and Hitler* by David Kertzer.
Go further to get different perspectives and explore further controversy about Pius XII – but keep in mind a comment I spotted online about Pius XII, "Saved more Jews during the Holocaust than any other single individual."

Eugenio Maria Giuseppe Giovanni Pacelli – who later became Pope Pius XII – was born in Rome on March 2, 1876.

He became pope on his birthday, March 2, 1939.

My birthday was in November that same year – November 10, 1939 – so he was the first pope in my lifetime.

He died in Castel Gandolfo on October 9, 1958. That was the pope's summer residence. It's cooler than Rome – but only 16 miles southeast of Rome. Pope Francis has been there, but doesn't use it – just like he doesn't use the Papal apartments for the Pope.

Pius XII did. He was that kind of pope – from a different era – and a different background – and definitely a different outlook.

Pius XII was thin and 6 feet tall. That's tall for an Italian. He didn't dominate the room – but he always looked official.

If anyone was ever prepared to be pope – it was Pope Pius XII – receiving training in law, diplomacy, concordats, documents, and decrees.

After his ordination to the priesthood, I noticed that he is listed as a curate in Chiesa Nuova – one of the better-known churches in Rome. That's where he made his First Communion and where he served as an altar boy. However, as a priest, he was only there for a very short time – about a year.

His family – and various relatives – held positions in the Church in Rome. In his biography, you find out that his father, grandfather, brother, and cousins were advisors to different popes, dean of the Roman Rota, and lay canon lawyers, among other roles. So he had witnessed the workings of the Church and saw potential for his own future as a cleric.

Early on, he worked as a secretary for influential figures in the Catholic Church. He also held titles such as Undersecretary and Secretary of State. He accompanied key individuals to funerals and participated in church agreements. He earned a doctorate in Canon Law. During discussions for agreements, he met Winston Churchill, the President of the United States, Franklin Delano Roosevelt, and various other high-ranking individuals.

While reading his life story, many questions arose for me. Who were his friends? What was he like at social gatherings and meetings? Was he an observer or an active participant? Would he be seen holding a drink? Did he go to bed early or late? Besides Italian and German, what other languages did he speak? What was it like to serve as pope during two world wars – especially in comparison to the years preceding and following World War I and II?

Next, I wanted to know his thoughts about the Church. I read that he considered calling for a Vatican Council II during his papacy, but ultimately did not. Why not? The pope who succeeded him, John XXIII, did call for one in 1961. What was his theological perspective? What were his theological leanings? I did come across a statement mentioning that as pope, "He reduced the Italian majority in the College of Cardinals in 1946."Internationally, he spent plenty of time in Germany – but he also got to the United States, England, South America, and various other places.

What I also found interesting was his ordination to the priesthood – just by himself – whereas most priests were ordained with classmates. He had started off his studies for the priesthood with others – but ended up living at home while going to the seminary for schooling. His sister, Elisabetta, said it was the food. So he got a dispensation to do some of his seminary work – while living at home.

I remember reading a biography of Sister Pascalina Lenhert. It was a book called La Pompessa. He had a lifetime friendship with her. It wasn't juicy – but it was a good way of hearing about the life and work of Pius XII. She was a friend and an advisor to him for a good part of his adult life.

In discussions about Pius XII, there were lots of comments about him not doing enough to defend the Jews in Europe and Germany against the Nazis. That is still pending. Some compliment him; some criticize him.

He was the Church I grew up in – until I was 18 in 1958. That was the year Pius XII died.

Then the Church and the world changed when we hit 1960.

Looking at his life and examining the thousands of documents – sermons – and 41 encyclicals – gives a good picture of the Church before John XXIII and the Second Vatican Council.

To me, he's the pope who triggers lots of questions –
lots of history – and lots of 'before' things changed.

Pope John XXIII

Angelo Giuseppe Roncalli – short, round, plump – followed Pius XII.

Wow, he was a surprise – and he knew it.

He was 76 years of age – elected pope on the 11th ballot on October 28, 1958 – perhaps as a caretaker pope.

We didn't have a sure pick right at that moment – but we did have time for an obvious star to appear on the horizon – but not a fat little short guy.

His life dates were November 25, 1881 till June 3, 1963.

He was the fourth of 13 children. His dad was a sharecropper farmer living in a small country village called Sotto il Monte. It's in the Bergamo province in the Lombardy region of Italy.

He became a priest on August 10, 1904 – and then served in a variety of different posts in the Catholic Church – in various places like France, Bulgaria, Greece, and Turkey.

Pius XII made him a cardinal – as well as the Patriarch of Venice – which was the door that opened his way to becoming Pope in 1958. Surprise.

Bigger surprise: he called for the Second Vatican Council in 1962. He didn't last until its ending – but he opened up the windows and doors of the church for fresh air to pour in. Luckily for us and for the Church, he kept a diary – which later was published as a book: Journal of a Soul.

His speeches and documents – along with the Second Vatican Documents – as well as all the moves he made before and after becoming the pope – show us what someone can do as pope.

He was known for having a sense of humor. Everyone has heard his best joke. When asked how many people work in the Vatican, his answer was, "About half of them." My favorite one was: "Dressed up as pope for the first time, he looked at himself in a big mirror and said, 'I'm going to be a disaster on television'."

That's one of the great secrets of life: the ability to laugh at oneself. Pope John XXIII certainly knew and had that gift.

He brought the church into the modern world. He brought the church into the mix of world politics as well as the ministry of world religions.

His experience in so many different posts and places – as well as what happened in the world in his lifetime – as well as being pope – helped *make him what Time magazine calls 'Man of the Year' in 1962.

Pope Paul VI

Pope Paul VI – born September 26, 1897 – died August 6, 1978.

That's a good long life – even better if you use your life – big time – sweet time – for others.

He was born in Concesio – a village in the Province of Brescia – in Lombardy – northern Italy – not that far from Milan.

His name had a long list of names: Giovanni Battista Enrico Antonio Maria Montini. That's something that happens regularly in Italy. It tells of the importance of family connections. Sometimes names are a long list of Saints' names. That shows faith connections.

We can ask of Pope Paul VI: what were the influences on his life that led him to eventually become Pope?

Key would be his connection to Pope Pius XII – serving in the Holy See's Secretariat of State – and then Pope Pius XII naming him to be the Archbishop of Milan – the largest

Italian diocese. This job led to his becoming Secretary of the Italian Bishops' Conference.

Of course, it all began with his first becoming a priest: May 29, 1920. What impact does having a priest in the family have on a family? I'm asking that in this book – especially with the next generation in our family no longer going to Mass. I wonder about that when it comes to weddings. As a priest, I did my nieces' weddings – but their kids are getting married in fields and barns and mansions – no priest added.

Do any of those kids say out loud, "Oh, I am a Catholic"?

Paul VI received a doctorate degree in Canon Law in Milan and also did some studies down in Rome at the Gregorian. So he got a good education. At times during his school years, he had serious bouts with sickness. Unfortunately, after ordination – he was not a parish priest – which is a very good educational experience for every priest.

Paul VI had two brothers. Francesco became a physician and Lodovico became a lawyer and politician. I don't know what their faith backgrounds sound like. I don't know how many nieces and nephews he has.

I'm sure a grandniece or a great-grandnephew would say at the barbershop or a dinner out, "Oh, I have a granduncle who was a pope."

His mom – Giudetta Alghisi – was from a noble family. His dad, Giorgio, was a journalist, a lawyer, and a member of the Italian Parliament. I wonder what conversations were like when they were growing up. I also wonder how many family gatherings they had as grown-ups. This is information I don't find in biographies of popes.

He only served in one Secretariat of State position outside of Italy. That was in Poland. It didn't work out too well. It could be nightmarish at times. That was in 1923. When he was pope, he wasn't allowed back into Poland for visits and celebrations at Marian shrines.

Pope John XXIII named him a cardinal – so with all those official jobs as background – he was on the short list of those who might get made a pope.

In his life as pope, he got a lot accomplished. He continued John XXIII's Second Vatican Council – which closed in 1965. Then the interpretations and implementations began. His up close and personal meetings and work for and with Pope Pius XII certainly helped him.

In 1968, he issued the famous encyclical – Humanae Vitae – on birth control. That document certainly drew lines in the sand – and put his name and picture in magazines and newspapers.

Like the other popes in modern times, Paul VI moved through the regular steps to be named a saint. Pope Francis canonized him on October 14, 2018.

Pope John Paul I

He had a great smile.

Albino Luciani was born on Oct. 17, 1912.

Pope John Paul the 1st – became the first pope to have that 'the 1st' in his name – especially when there was a John Paul II.

John Paul the first lasted only 33 days, making him the pope with the shortest term in the long line of 263 popes. Of course – with such a sudden death – rumors that he was murdered appeared on the scene. If interested, David Yallop published a book in 1984 about a possible murder. It was entitled, *In God's Name*. John Cornwall, a British historian published a counter account, called *A Thief in the Night*.

The best evidence suggests 'No Murder'.

1978 was the year of the three popes.

By taking two names – John and Paul – Albino connected himself to the two popes before him. John XXIII made him a bishop and Paul VI made him a cardinal.

He choose 'Humility' as his motto – just one word.

He got the nick name 'The Smiling Pope'. "*Il Papa del Sorriso*." – as well as 'The Smile of God' – "*Il Sorriso di Dio*." He certainly had a great smile.

But underneath that smile a psychiatrist said, "He was scared."

He died – probably – of a heart attack – at the age of 65.

He had his critics – people thinking he was going to make significant reforms in the church, changes that made some nervous. I would assume that is a given for every new pope.

A higher up in the church said, "They have elected Peter Sellers."

Albino Luciani was from the town of Forno di Canale in the Veneto region of Northern Italy.

His dates: October 17, 1912 – August 26, 1978.

He didn't want to be elected Pope.

I remember being stationed in Tobyhanna, Pennsylvania, at the time. I came down to the chapel for morning prayer at 7:30. Leo, my boss, said, "The Pope died."

Half asleep, I said, "I know!"

Knowing I didn't know, Leo said, "No. The new pope."

"Ooooh – wow – whoa," I said.

And Leo smiling said, "And I didn't buy the new picture."

We had pictures of the pope in all our houses.

He chose John Paul as his pope's name because John XXIII named him a bishop, and Paul VI named him a cardinal.

He had a full life. It's too bad we didn't get to see what he would have done as pope.

His father, Giovanni, was a bricklayer.

He tried to join the Jesuits – but wasn't accepted.

He became a diocesan priest, starting as a parish priest in Forno de Canale, where he came from.

Next, he became a teacher in the seminary, teaching theology, canon law, and sacred art. Then he began working on his doctorate in theology from the Pontifical Gregorian University. His superiors in the seminary didn't want him in Rome studying, so they got him a dispensation from having to study there.

His doctorate was entitled *The Origin of the Human Soul* according to Antonio Rosmini. He completed it, receiving a magna cum laude degree in 1947.

Next came nominations to become a bishop – but poor health got in the way.

He wrote a book, *Catechesis in Crumbs*. He wanted to teach the truths of the Catholic faith – in plain and simple language. I've never seen that book in English.

In December of 1958 he was named bishop of Vittorio Veneto by Pope John XXIII.

He took as his bishop's motto just one word: 'Humility'.

In December of 1969 he was named Patriarch of Venice by Pope Paul VI.

In March of 1973 he was named a Cardinal.

In January of 1976 another book of his writings came out. It was simply a collection of letters he imagined – sent to famous people; such as King David, Charles Dickens, Teresa of Avila, Pinocchio, Figaro, Goethe, Chesterton, Jesus and others. It was called *Illustrissimi – The Illustrious*. It came out in English once he was made pope.

Even though he had a great smile, he could also have perceived enemies – especially from people who didn't like his take on money, marriage, divorce, donations to the poor, and who makes the appointments of priests.

For starters, he had a six-point plan on what to do as pope. We'll never know how this would have happened.

To renew the church through the policies implemented by Vatican II.

To revise canon law.

To remind the church of its duty to preach the Gospel.

To promote church unity without watering down doctrine.

To promote dialogue.

To encourage world peace and social justice.

Pope John Paul II He

He…

He was born on May 18, 1920 in Wadowice – a small city – in the Second Polish Republic. It's about 31 miles to Krakow. His name: Karol Józef Wojtyła.

He was the youngest of three children. His parents – Karol Wojtyla Sr. and Emilia Kaczprpwsla were dead by the time he was 21 – as well as his sister and brother. His sister. Olga, died before Karol was born. His brother Edmund died early on – when Karol was around 12 years of age. His brother was a doctor.

He had a schoolteacher for a mom. She died from a heart attack and kidney failure in 1929. Karol was 8 years old at the time. His dad was a non-commissioned army officer who died in 1941.

He was elected pope in 1978. I remember asking out loud when I heard his name for the first time, "What nationality is that?" I thought for a second and asked: "Is that Japanese?"

He learned at least 15 languages.

He went to Marcin Wadowita High School in Wadowice.

He then enrolled in Krakow's Jagiellonian University in 1938. He also entered a school for drama. The Nazi's forced

Jagiellonian University to close not too long after that – but it opened up again after the war.

He began to work in a quarry from 1940 to 1944.

He also worked in the Solvay chemical factory to earn a living. It was a way to avoid being deported to Germany.

He also took up studies to become a priest in 1942 – in secret. He also did some theatrical work – secret – as well.

He continued his studies in Krakow Seminary when it reopened – as well as being part of Jagiellonian University when it reopened.

He said some time in his 60s, "I was not at my mother's death, I was not at my brother's death, I was not at my father's death." He added, "At 20, I had already lost all the people I loved."

He was ordained a priest on November 1, 1946.

He was sent to Rome after that. He studied under Garrigou-Lagrange – the French Dominican. He got a Ph.D. from the Pontifical University of St. Thomas Aquinas in 1948. He covered the theme of faith in the works of St. John of the Cross.

He did various types of pastoral ministry for Polish immigrants from France, Belgium and Holland – when he had the opportunity to do so.

He went back to Poland in 1948 – working in different parishes in Krakow – up till 1951. He was also chaplain to university students.

He also took further studies in philosophy and theology – when he had the opportunity. The Jagiellonian University opened up again.

He also became a professor of moral theology and social ethics in the major seminary of Krakow and in the Faculty of Theology of Lublin.

He was made an Auxiliary bishop of Krakow Poland from 1958 till 1964.

He became the Archbishop of Krakow from 1964 till 1978.

He was in on the drafting of a prime document of the Second Vatican Council: *Gaudium et Spes* – as well as being there for the whole council – 1962–1965.

He was named a cardinal on June 26, 1967

He was elected the 263rd pope in 1978. He was the first non-Italian pope since Adrian VI in the 16th century. He was the second-longest-serving pope – almost 27 years – after Pope Pius IX in modern history.

He visited 317 of the city's 333 parishes as bishop of Rome.

He visited 129 countries as pope.

He had 19 World Youth Days – as pope.

He also had World Meetings as Families.

He met people in the millions as pope

He was close to Jewish people all through his life.

He helped end communism in Poland and much of Europe.

He died in Vatican City – on April 2nd 2005.

He was beatified on 1 May 2011.

He was canonized a saint on April 27, 2014.

He had for his motto and life theme: '*Totus tuus*'. He certainly was all to all that he met.

Pope Benedict XVI

It's interesting that the one thing that Pope Benedict will be most famous for will be his resignation from being pope on February 28, 2013.

He was the first pope to do that since Gregory XII in 1415. Before that Celestine V resigned in 1294 – but he did it like Benedict as his own choice.

On September 4, 2020 – he became the pope who lived the longest in years of life. His brother Georg died at the age 96.

Benedict followed Pope John Paul II who was pope for 26 years. Benedict was pope from April 19, 2005 till February 28, 2013.

His mom and dad had 3 kids. Joseph Aloisius, the youngest, who became the pope. His brother, Georg, was also a priest. Then there was their sister, Maria, who never got married.

They lived up there in Bavaria, Germany. His mom's family were originally from South Tyrol [Italy].

He was born on April 16, 1927

When he hit 14, Joseph had to join the Hitler Youth. Since March of 1939 all 14-year-old boys had to do this. Like his father he was anti-Nazi. His father was a policeman

– who got demotions and had problems because he was against Nazism.

A cousin – a 14-year-old boy was murdered by the Nazis – because he had Down Syndrome.

Joseph, in 1943, while still in seminary, was drafted into the German anti-aircraft corps. He also then trained in the German infantry. As the Allied front drew closer to his post in 1945, he deserted back to his family's home in Traunstein. His unit had ceased to exist. American troops established a headquarters in the Ratzinger household. As a German soldier, he was interned in a prisoner of war camp. He was released a few months later at the end of the war in May 1945.

He was ordained a priest on June 29, 1951.

He was consecrated a bishop on May 28, 1977.

He was Archbishop of Munich and Freising from 1977 to 1982.

He was created a cardinal on June 27, 1977.

He was named pope on April 18, 2005.

Benedict wrote three encyclicals: *God Is Love; Saved by Hope* and *Love in Truth*. If you want their names in Latin they are: *Deus Caritas Est, Spe Salvi,* et *Caritas In Veritate.*

He resigned from being a pope on February 28, 2013.

In the second half of the 20th Century, he was known around the Catholic world – as a leading theologian.

He did a lot of academic writing – as well as teaching in leading European Catholic institutes.

Two things that he asked for before his death was forgiveness for anyone he hurt and thanks to God for all his blessings.

He died December 31, 2022 in the Mater Ecclesiae
Monastery in Vatican City, Rome. His age: 95 years of life.

Pope Francis

Pope Francis, Cardinal Jorge Mario Bergoglio, was born in Buenos Aires, Argentina on December 17, 1936. He was elected pope in 2013. He emphasized poverty, the environment, and immigrant rights. He was the first Jesuit elected pope and the first Argentinian as well. He established a commission to address clerical sexual abuse.

Jorge Mario Bergoglio had a remarkable name. He is the 266th pope in the Catholic Church. He was born on December 17, 1936 in Flores, a neighborhood of Buenos Aires, Argentina.

His father, Mario, was an accountant who was born in Italy. He left Italy in 1929 and moved to Argentina to escape Mussolini. His mother, Regina Silvori, was born in Argentina. Both of them had Italian heritage.

They had 5 children, with Jorge being the oldest.

He received a good education.

He worked as a bouncer, loved to tango, worked as a janitor, and was also a chemist.

He became a Jesuit, a Catholic priest, the archbishop of Buenos Aires, and a cardinal, which eventually led to his election as pope.

The word was that he had the second most votes when Benedict was elected pope. So when Benedict resigned, he was next – and took the name of Pope Francis of Assisi in March of 2013.

He became pope at the age of 76, so health issues are a concern in the wings.

Compared to Pius XII and Benedict, Pope Francis is certainly less formal. He lives in a papal guesthouse instead of the regular papal apartments.

He continues the papal views on celibacy, abortion, and women priests – but based on comments and practices, we can expect more discussion on women's roles and positions in our church. He is definitely not a harsh critic when it comes to gay and LGBT individuals.

He has traveled to Germany, Chile, Ireland, and various other places – both Jesuit and non-Jesuit. He has had his own stories and struggles.

Writers like to highlight his fondness for the image of Mary – with the title of Untier of Knots – which can be found in Augsburg, Germany. He introduced that image to the people of Argentina.

He encountered issues from time to time in both Argentina and the worldwide church. Unlike most of his predecessors in his role as pope, he has his enemies.

He chose as his episcopal motto: *Miserando atque eligendo.* – "Having mercy, he called him." He took it from Saint Bede's homily on Matthew 9: 9–13. Francis liked the words and the message:

Because he saw him through the eyes of mercy and chose him.

Encyclicals

In the Catholic Church, encyclicals are letters from the Pope.

In my opinion, a better title would be *A Statement from the Pope.*

An encyclical is an official document to be circulated and shared.

You can spot the word 'cycle' in it. We should know that from the word 'recycle' which we hear at least 3 times every week.

So, as Catholics, we understand the meaning of the word 'encyclical' when it is used for the Pope's letters.

When priests or deacons use the word 'encyclical' in a sermon or a comment in a church bulletin, I bet it evokes an unconscious 'What'?

You would not hear the words 'ice cream' or 'electric razor' in an encyclical – but if you did, you would know what they are. You can imagine them – but spiritual 'stuff' is much more difficult to grasp.

Popes or their communication teams send out these letters to Catholics during their time as Pope.

They are not poetry or storytelling.

Humanae Vitae – the 1968 Encyclical – by Pope Paul VI – is perhaps the most widely read of all the papal encyclicals in the last 82 years. It was about Birth Control. It said, "No!" It was conveying the message that "Catholics believe that people are more important than things."

If you are interested in this subject, you can search it on Google. Type in a Pope's name – and then add the word 'encyclicals'.

Under Paul VI, a list of 26 encyclicals would appear. Then you can choose any one of those encyclicals and read it.

They have some interesting titles like *Mitt songerer Jurgen* by Pius XI or *Mater et Magister* by John 23rd.

During my seminary days, I had to write a term paper on Humanae Generis – an encyclical from Pius XII. It also had the theme of 'No' in it – a bit too much at times – when it comes to theological expressions or musings. The documents of Vatican II would be a bit more liberal.

For anyone wanting to know more about the teachings and theology of the Catholic Church – knowing about encyclicals – for example, the ten most important encyclicals of the past 100 years – would be a wise interest and intellectual investment.

Computers are a useful tool – and viewing and reading encyclicals online – is free of charge.

Models of The Church

In the early 1970s, I was working hard as a priest, but I was not reading enough theology and spirituality to stay up to date.

I happened to meet a priest at the San Alfonso Retreat House in Long Branch, New Jersey, who had experienced the same concern and question. A Protestant minister suggested that he take some courses at the nearby Princeton Theological Seminary.

He decided to give it a try. Princeton Theological was only 20 minutes away from his parish. In two years, he obtained a Master's Degree in Theology (ThM). He considered it a wise decision.

I decided to check it out as well. Princeton Theological was only an hour away. I enrolled, and in two years, I earned my third Master's degree, also in Theology – a ThM.

During the second year, they invited some Catholic theologians to join their faculty. I was simply looking for knowledgeable professors offering interesting courses. I took a course by Father Avery Dulles, a Jesuit, called "Models of the Church."

It turned out to be a good decision.

There were approximately 25 people taking Dulles' course, and during that semester, someone remarked, "He must be writing a book on this material."

Sure enough his course became a book that did very well: *Models of the Church.*

I'm weak in analytical skills – but I was able to get my mind on the gist of what he was saying and trying to figure out. Let me attempt to explain.

First of all: be aware of models.

For example…

A couple gets married. They live in a rented apartment for a few years and start having a family. They figure out that they want a home – with a back porch and a backyard.

They find the perfect house that they have in mind. Next, they start wondering about furniture. They go to about 5 furniture stores and find themselves in total disagreement about the type of furniture they want. Finally, a salesman asks, "Do you want modern furniture or old-fashioned furniture?"

That question turns the light on for them. Eureka!

He wants modern; she wants old-fashioned.

The first question they should have been asking was: What model do we have in mind for the kind of furniture we want to buy?

In a way, it's the same question when it comes to church. What model do I have in mind for the church I want to be a member of? What am I looking for?

Many people go to the church their parents gave them – and on and on and on, back to someone who started them on their trajectory path.

People grow and go to the church of their roots.

Then some people drop out. Or they change to the church of their spouse. Or they find a church that appeals to their needs.

Avery Dulles came up with 5 models of the Catholic Church. I understand 3 out of the 5 models. I understand 1, 4 and 5.

The first model is the institution. I need an organization. I need structure. The Catholic Church certainly has that. Some say it's a pyramid. The pope is on top. Next come the bishops – in charge of dioceses. Next comes the parish with the pastor.

It's a lot more than that – but seeing and knowing the structure and the system helps. Some like it; some don't.

The second model is the Mystical Body of Christ. I need the structure – but I also want the Spirit behind and underneath and within the structure: Christ.

Paul – Saint Paul – in his First Letter to the Corinthians describes this model best for me. He borrowed the model from the way he heard a Greek city being described. It has a head. We need someone with brains. We need leaders. We need someone who is handy. We need people who do the footwork and on and on and on. Head, heart, hands…

So that's the second model of the church. It's spelled out in the encyclical called Mystici Corporis – the Body of Christ.

It's like a human body.

The third model is the one I can never explain. The Church is a Sacrament – an outward sign – that gives grace. It's both outward – but it's also inward. It's visible and invisible. It's that inward, invisible stuff that I don't get.

The fourth model is a group of people who need to gather regularly and explore its sacred words and roots – and then put them into practice.

It's Bible-based. It's a group of people who meet on a regular basis to ponder its Bible stories, sayings, and teachings.

The fifth model is a group of people who feed, serve, and care for others. So we need people to start hospitals and food kitchens. It's all about serving others.

Dulles gave us a semester of classes on figuring out the blueprints for a church. Then out came his red-colored book – which helped people figure out – what they wanted from the church.

There are other ways of describing all this – but KISS. Keep It Simple, Stupid.

I hope I have done it that way – in this book – at least a tiny bit.

Communion

Sometimes people ask priests about receiving communion.

What are the rules regarding who can and cannot receive communion?

Sometimes the best answer is to make an appointment with a priest – to talk – to listen – to discover – to learn – while simply sitting there with a priest.

I would also suggest my old rule: attend a Sunday Mass. Observe. Listen to. Get a good sense of the priest who is celebrating the Mass. Ask yourself: could I have a conversation with this person? Does this person seem like a good listener? Or is he someone who would be unapproachable? "Grr! Grr! Grr!"

If a priest addresses this topic in a sermon – sometimes it can cause uproar or upset. Other times, it can be the best sermon of the year. It could bring people to reflect on several important life issues.

Imagine someone who hasn't received communion for 50 years – because they were in a broken marriage and they believed the rule was: "Now you can't receive communion."

They go to church and the opening song is, "All are welcome in this place." Then the sermon echoes that message.

I would hope that a diocese could make the question of receiving communion a topic for a diocesan meeting for priests and deacons.

I would hope that a diocesan meeting on the topic of receiving communion would then involve: including members – men and women of the diocese – in meetings on this topic.

We also need the bishops of the different dioceses of a country to address this topic. Then we need to bring up this topic to the Church.

We also need the theologians of our Church to convene and discuss this topic.

By doing this, we should discover that we are not all in agreement on this matter.

A priest in Parish A says that people who do not oppose abortion should not receive communion.

A priest in Parish B says that politicians and public officials who vote for abortion should be denied Holy Communion.

A priest in Parish C says that anyone who, in conscience, wants to receive communion should be allowed to.

A preacher in Parish D says, "Jesus says, 'Let the one without sin cast the first stone. Let the one without sin gather stones to build walls to have a place for non-sinners.'"

A parishioner in Parish E says, "If you are going to prevent people from receiving communion, who decides which sins we are talking about here?"

A woman in St. Louis says, "I thought Jesus said, 'I eat with sinners and dine with them.'"

A pope in Rome gives communion to all those who line up in his communion line.

A preacher in Parish F says, "Take and eat. This is my body. Take and drink. This is my blood."

A priest reading this says, "This is heresy!"

And Jesus, the Bread of Life, eagerly desires to enter into the hearts and minds of those who hunger for him.

Invitation

Jesus enjoyed telling stories.

Jesus enjoyed extending invitations to people. He enjoyed speaking to those who climbed trees just to catch a glimpse of him – because they were too short. He enjoyed conversing with people at wells. If you read the gospels, you will read about all kinds of invitations.

You are invited…

Once, he told a story about a king whose son was getting married.

A grand banquet was planned, but no one showed up.

So he said, "Forget about those who do not want to come."

He said that because people would experience hell when they did not experience what he wanted to give them.

Then he added, "Go out to anyone and everyone – anywhere and everywhere – to those who are hungry – to those who are thirsty – and invite them to the banquet."

"To those who do not want me – to those who want to spend their lives wailing and complaining – grumbling and grinding their teeth – okay – that's your move and that's your choice."

Christianity – Catholicism – Christ – is a banquet.

You are invited.

If you do not choose me, the people in the next village might.

And that is the history of the world.

And that is the history [his-story] of Jesus Christ.

Your choice. Your move.

A long time ago, I was sitting in a Catholic grammar school classroom. A priest walked in and told us he was a Redemptorist missionary in Brazil. I listened – a fifth-grade kid listened. It sounded fascinating.

He then said, "If anyone is interested in considering becoming a priest, raise your hand."

I raised my hand and that became my history. I laugh because people laugh at me when I tell them that I went away to a prep high school at the age of 13. What would they think if I told them I was thinking about becoming a priest at the age of 8 or 9?

Maybe nothing, as little kids love to tell their parents and grandparents that they want to be firefighters or astronauts or doctors or nurses when they grow up.

I never did get assigned to Brazil. My classmate Larry did. He passed away last year at 82. I am still going.

My first assignment was at Most Holy Redeemer Church on the Lower East Side of New York City. It was from February 1967 to 1969. It was a time when teenagers were flocking away from their parents to the East Village of Manhattan, New York City.

It was the beginning of my true education – discovering what made people think – what people truly desired. I was told, "We are going to place you in a parish so that you can come down to earth." And I did.

I once read in a book that the famous American priest, Andrew Greely, had a similar experience to mine. He said he raised his hand in the fourth grade. Then he added, "I never put my hand down."

I ended up working and living in New Jersey, Washington D.C., Pennsylvania, Wisconsin, upper and lower New York State, Ohio, and Maryland.

I was stationed in St. Mary's Parish, Annapolis, Maryland, for 17 years [2002-2019]. For one of my birthdays, the school staff gave me a book: Devotions, by Mary Oliver.

In that book, I found a poem that expressed what I was doing with my life in poetic words. I was getting on a donkey and traveling around, telling people about Jesus.

Here is that poem. So let me close my book with these words from the poet, Mary Oliver. It is me. At least, I hope it is.

The Poet Thinks About The Donkey

On the outskirts of Jerusalem
the donkey waited.
Not especially brave, or filled with understanding,
he stood and waited.
How horses, turned out into the meadow,
leap with delight!
How doves, released from their cages,
chatter away, splashed with sunlight.
But the donkey, tied to a tree as usual, waited.
Then he let himself be led away.
Then he let the stranger mount.
Never had he seen such crowds!
And I wonder if he at all imagined what was to happen.
Still he was what he had always been: small, dark, obedient.
I hope, finally, he felt brave.
I hope, finally, he loved the man who rode so lightly upon
him,
as he had lifted one dusty hoof and stepped, as he had to,
forward.